9012   23

W9-BKZ-507

DOUBTING THOMAS

DOUBTING THOMAS

Christology in Story Form

JOHN B. COBB, JR.

CROSSROAD • NEW YORK

This book is an expression of the interest of "Process and Faith" to provide serious theological materials in a readable form for a wide public. Process and Faith is a program of the Center for Process Studies, located on the campus of the School of Theology at Claremont, Claremont CA 91711-3199. Readers interested in learning more about the program are encouraged to write to that address.

1990

The Crossroad Publishing Company
370 Lexington Avenue, New York, NY 10017

Printed in the United States of America

Library of Congress Cataloging-in-Publication Data

Cobb, John B.
    Doubting Thomas : Christology in story form / John B. Cobb, Jr.
      p. cm.
    Includes bibliographical references.
    ISBN 0-8245-1033-X
    1. Jesus Christ — Fiction.   I. Title.   II. Title: Christology in story form.
    PS3553.0186D6   1990
    813'.54 — dc20
                                          89-38794
                                              CIP

Contents

• 1 •

After Church—
Sunday Morning

THOMAS ATHERTON WAS SHAKEN. His life had always proceeded in an orderly way. He had made decisions carefully, and once he made them, he carried through despite setbacks and obstacles. But this time. . . .

He had made the decision as carefully and thoughtfully as usual. He and his wife, Mary, had prayed about it. This position as chaplain's assistant at the regional university of his denomination had seemed an ideal way to meet the requirement for an internship during his seminary career. He had met Janet Levovsky, the chaplain, and he had liked her. She was warm and caring and generous with her time. His first month as a chaplain-intern had been rewarding.

But listening to her sermon this Sunday morning had confirmed a growing suspicion. Chaplain Levovsky was not a believing Christian! Hard as it was to see how this could be true, the denomination had placed in this important position a minister who did not believe that Jesus was the Son of God. How could he do his internship under a supervisor who was not really a Christian at all? Would he have to ask for a new assignment? What a pain and hassle that would be! Would the seminary agree with his reasons? Was it already too late?

Thomas felt anger rising in him against the chaplain, but also against Prof. Smith, who handled placements at the seminary, and against the church and the university, too. It wasn't fair to put a seminary student in such a position. And even worse, it was simply wrong to have the church represented on the university campus by such a person! But feeling the anger upset him all the more. It wasn't right to be angry, especially not in church. The anger blotted out the love he knew he ought to feel even for those who had put him in this dilemma.

Mary noticed Thomas's agitation. When the benediction had been pronounced she asked, "What's the matter, Tom?"

Thomas started to brush off the question with an "Oh, nothing really!" but he thought better of it. He had relied on Mary's understanding and counsel ever since they married after the junior year of college. Indeed, he depended on her in a lot of ways. They had struggled through the last year of college together, but he didn't know how he could have gone to seminary at all if she hadn't taken a full-time job as a secretary. This year, too, she was the chief bread-winner. He tried to help out at home, but she was the chief cook and housekeeper, too. And still she was interested in his studies and in what he thought! He thanked God daily for leading him to her.

Even so, he rarely talked with her about problems and uncertainties of a purely theological sort, partly because he loved her serene faith and didn't want to disturb it. Partly, also, the problems didn't seem very important. They would work themselves out, he felt sure, in the course of his studies. But this time, he realized, he was more upset than usual. He needed Mary's reassurance and counsel.

"That sermon bothered me," he answered. "It sounded

as though Jesus were just another person very much like us, as if he were a child of God in just the same sense that we are. I don't see how a Christian preacher can talk like that!"

"I guess there *was* a lot of emphasis on how human Jesus was," Mary agreed, "but I don't see why that should upset you. No preacher can say everything every Sunday. When I was growing up my Sunday school teachers often pictured Jesus as a very nice teacher who loved little children. But I'm sure they believed in his divinity. Maybe next Sunday Chaplain Levovsky will preach on Jesus' divinity."

"But we've been listening to her sermons ever since we came here for my internship five weeks ago," Thomas complained, "and I never hear anything about Jesus' divinity. I'm not at all sure she believes in it. I don't see how I can go on working under her if she's not even a Christian!"

By this time they had slipped out the side door to avoid speaking to Chaplain Levovsky and were well on their way home. Mary felt sure that Thomas was wrong. She was confident that all ministers believed in the divinity of Jesus. She had heard enough talk among the students at the seminary to know that they went through a lot of confusion and doubts as they studied the many different theologies. Some students, she thought, went too far — really left the Christian fold. But she was sure that most of them would get straightened out before they graduated. The others would drop out or, if they sought ordination, would be refused by the church. To be an ordained minister in a mainstream denomination certainly must mean that one is an orthodox believer! Finally she said, "Why don't you talk with her about it? I'm sure you'll feel better."

• 2 •

The Chaplain's Office —
Tuesday Morning

"COME IN, THOMAS," called Janet Levovsky, "how are things going with you and Mary?"

"Thanks, we're comfortably settled, and we both like our jobs."

"You seemed troubled when you called yesterday to ask for an appointment. I was afraid something had gone wrong."

It was hard for Thomas to say what was bothering him. He had never raised this kind of question with a professor. As his supervisor, he felt toward her in much the same way. He didn't want to seem to be critical. But the chaplain was waiting. "I really liked yesterday's sermon. It's always a treat to hear you preach. You come through as yourself and what you say comes out of your own experience. Maybe it's for just that reason that I have to take it so seriously."

"That's good to hear, but I take it that I said something you didn't like. I really do appreciate your coming to tell me about it. Sometimes I hear about criticisms at second and third hand, and I feel so frustrated. This way I'll understand better. What was wrong with my sermon?" She knew she was becoming defensive and regretted it.

"I guess what I'm concerned about is not what you do say so much as what you don't say. Yesterday the point seemed to be how human Jesus was, how much like us. And as I think back over your other sermons, that seems quite consistent with what you've said before. I know it's right to say that Jesus was truly human, of one substance with us in his humanity, but surely that's only a part of the message. Surely Jesus was divine, too. Isn't that the main point — that Jesus was uniquely divine?"

So that was it, thought Janet, another conservative on her hands. Indeed, seminary students seemed to be getting more conservative all the time. Meanwhile, she was becoming less patient with those old problems. There was so much the church needed to be doing for peace, for liberation, for mutual understanding among the peoples and religions! And still these hang-ups on ancient dogma! But this time, at least, the conservative came to talk — not to snipe at her behind her back. And he seemed really to be asking questions, not giving her an exam for orthodoxy. She resolved to be open with him.

"Thomas, I think I understand what's bothering you. And all the more I appreciate your coming to talk with me about it. You and I have come to the church by quite different paths, I'm sure, and so we think about our faith quite differently, but I'm confident we can work together, even if we have to agree to disagree on some matters. You've picked up bits and pieces about me from earlier conversations and from my sermons, but let me tell you the story of my faith-pilgrimage a little more fully. Then you'll understand better where I'm coming from."

Both of them began to relax a bit. Chaplain Levovsky was no longer defensive, and Thomas was eager to understand her better.

"I grew up outside organized religion. My parents thought of themselves as agnostics. They ridiculed what they understood to be Christian dogma and led me to wonder how any intelligent person could be a Christian. Occasionally I listened to radio and TV preachers, and that only confirmed in me my parents' rejection of faith."

"Some of that media stuff is pretty bad," Thomas agreed.

"That's what I thought," Janet responded, eager to underscore any agreement. She continued, "The only thing that cut against this attitude was my fondness for my father's sister, Margaret. She didn't talk much about it, but I knew she was a Christian, and I loved to be with her. Occasionally when I was in high school I would spend a weekend with her. She would ask me whether I wanted to go with her Sunday morning. The first time or two I declined, but later I went with her to her discussion group. What I found there had nothing to do with the strange ideas about how three persons were one God or about Armageddon or miracles. Instead, I found a group of caring and sensitive adults who were interested in me in a way I had never experienced before. I felt that I could tell them what I really thought, and off-the-wall as some of those ideas were, they took them seriously. They thought of themselves as a group of seekers for spiritual truth supporting one another along the way."

Thomas remembered a college group he had been in that had some of that feel. But he had been a little too sure of his beliefs to be quite at home there. For the first time, he felt a pang of regret.

"That group talked about all kinds of things," Chaplain Levovsky continued, "much of it not specifically Christian. But sometimes they stopped to pray, thanking God for being with them or asking God's special blessing on one of their members. I had no idea what they meant by 'God,' but what they did seemed genuine."

Thomas noticed that there were tears in the chaplain's eyes. Clearly these were very precious memories.

"My aunt became sick, and after a long illness she died. During her illness we went as a family to visit her every few weeks, and between times my parents let me go alone. Even in her pain and weakness she was for me a tower of strength. I would ask her sometimes about God and about Jesus. Her answers were very simple, naive, I suppose, but they redirected my life. When I think of Christ I think of Aunt Margaret.

"My parents were astonished at the new course my life took — most of all when I told them I wanted to go to seminary. But they prided themselves on their tolerance, and they were relieved that I didn't go in for what they considered the hocus-pocus and absurdities of the Christianity they had known. They haven't become Christians themselves, but they don't object much to my variety of faith. We get along well together."

"So the deity of Jesus and the atonement and the resurrection haven't been important to you?" Thomas asked.

"I'm afraid my position is more extreme than that, Thomas. I think they *are* important, but they seem more like important obstacles that prevent people from following Jesus than like important aspects of faith itself."

Thomas was moved but he was even more troubled than when he first came in. "But then what do you believe?" he cried.

"I believe lots of things, Thomas," she replied gently. "I believe that the spirit I found in my aunt's discussion group back in my high school days was the Holy Spirit, and I try to serve that Spirit always. I've learned how closely the community that grew up around Jesus and especially after he was no longer with the disciples is bound up with that

Spirit. And I've learned that that Spirit is truly God with us. I have learned to call that Spirit Christ."

"Is that all?" Thomas blurted out.

Chaplain Levovsky was hurt; she had thought that Thomas was following her with more understanding. But she checked her renewed feelings of defensiveness. She could see that Thomas was genuinely troubled and needed time and help to assimilate what she was saying. "That's a great deal," she answered. "If you had ever experienced the thought world and the feeling world of unbelief in which I grew up, you would see how very important those beliefs are. I have known redemption through that Christ, and I try to help others find it as well. For me nothing is more important than that."

It seemed there was not much more to say. What for her was an obstacle to faith was for him its very content. In terms of all he believed, she was no Christian. Yet sitting there, hearing her story, he felt the genuineness of her faith. Could there be more than one way to being Christian? Could one who did not believe in Jesus' deity still be a believer? "Thank you," he said, "for sharing with me. I admit I'm very confused. I'll have to think about it. May I come again if I have more questions later on?"

"Of course," she said. But as she let him out she felt the return of a deep sadness. Sometimes she wondered whether the Spirit from whom and for whom she lived was different, after all, from the Spirit of whom the Scriptures witness. Maybe those who attacked her were right. Maybe Christianity was what her parents rejected rather than what her aunt had lived and taught her to love.

• 3 •

At Home —
Tuesday Noon

THOMAS HAD A SIMPLE LUNCH READY when Mary came home. They were both pleased that their campus jobs enabled them to eat lunch together several days each week. But when Mary saw Thomas she knew the conversation with the chaplain had not gone well. Thomas would need to de-brief with her, as they liked to call it. As soon as he had said grace, she asked him to tell her what Chaplain Levovsky had said.

"She told me how she became a Christian," Thomas replied. "I was really moved by her story. I like her more than ever."

"But you don't seem very happy about it! What did she say about the deity of Jesus?"

"Well, she didn't say so in so many words, but the truth is she doesn't believe in it at all. What I thought I heard her saying in those sermons is what she really means! She wants to free us from all the traditional beliefs."

It was Mary's turn to be shocked, really shocked. "But how could she be ordained to preach if she doesn't believe the church's teaching? And how could the seminary approve her as your supervisor for this intern year? You must have misunderstood her."

"No," Thomas said sadly. "I'm quite sure I didn't misunderstand. She went to the most liberal seminary of our denomination. And I realize now that some of what I have read and heard in my seminary is more like what she said than I had taken in before. I've just been assuming that everybody really believed the way I did and ignoring the threatening ideas. Chaplain Levovsky states them so directly I can't ignore them."

Thomas's reply was far from reassuring. To Mary what it meant to be Christian was quite clear. It involved a certain way of life and definite beliefs. On unimportant matters Christians could argue if they chose, but on essentials there must be full agreement. Otherwise how could they worship and work together? She did not go around hunting for heresy. Far from it. To all who called themselves Christian she attributed the beliefs that went with being Christian. But here was Thomas reporting that a respected pastor did not accept the core beliefs of the Christian faith. And worse yet, Mary feared, Thomas himself seemed shaken! A chaplain-supervisor had no business undermining the faith of interns.

"You're in a difficult position, honey. But you will let the seminary officials know, won't you? They won't want their students supervised by a chaplain who is not a believer. If it's really as you say, I hope you can get reassigned quickly."

Thomas suddenly regretted having told Mary what the chaplain had said, or at least of having put it so strongly. Mary was so decisive! That was part of what he liked about her. He often found it hard to make decisions himself, and he needed her clarity — the way she came to the point at once. Without her he doubted he could have ever finally decided for the ministry. She hadn't pushed him. She had just listened to him and helped him see that that was what he felt called to do. Once he was clear about that, she helped him brush aside all objections and quickly apply to seminary.

But this time she was moving ahead of him and in a direction he dreaded. She was assuming that he believed just as she did. Why shouldn't she? He had shared a lot of what he learned in seminary, but not in a way that would let her know what was really happening to him. That was partly because he wasn't sure himself, and it was hard to put into words. But it was also because he knew it would upset her.

What *was* happening? Looking back he could just begin to describe it to himself. The study of the Bible and the history of the church made everything about Christianity seem less fixed. For example, he still believed in the Virgin Birth, but when his New Testament professor pointed out that the genealogies in both Matthew and Luke seemed to assume that Jesus' descent was through Joseph and that the doctrine of Mary's virginity played no role in Paul's letters, he found it harder to suppose that this belief was essential to Christianity. He had come to accept the idea that Jesus' divinity was not dependent on Mary's virginity, although he himself continued to affirm the Virgin Birth. But he had not told Mary of his changing attitude. After all, he had not changed his own belief; so there had not seemed to be anything to tell.

He saw now that this softening process had gone farther than he had realized. It had become harder and harder to draw clear boundaries. Confronted by Chaplain Levovsky's story, he was confused. Could that, too, be Christian? Part of him wanted to say, "Yes!" But Mary didn't share that part of him and would not understand it — at least not right away.

"I don't know what to do, darling," Thomas finally

said. "I don't feel right about reporting officially what she told me in private. And I *am* confused. Maybe there *is* room in the church for people like her. I've found a number of students here who respond well to her and say they've never been able to make sense of Christianity before. At least it's a place to start — a point of contact."

"How could the denial of Jesus' deity be a point of contact for the gospel?" Mary replied sharply. To her this made no sense at all. But she saw that he was not ready to act and that it would do no good to push him. "Why don't you talk it over with Chan-Hie?"

Chan-Hie Park was the other intern working with Chaplain Levovsky that year. He came from another seminary, he was single, and he had a quite different role on campus, working especially with international students. Mary and Thomas were not yet well acquainted with him, but they respected what they had seen of his work. Thomas thought Mary's advice was good.

• 4 •

The Campus Cafeteria —
Wednesday Noon

"It's good to see you again, Chan-Hie. How's your work going?"

"The short answer is 'fine,' " Chan-Hie replied. "If you want the truth, it will take all afternoon to tell you. How is it with yours?"

"Mixed," said Thomas. "Really, I'm enjoying it, and Chaplain Levovsky has been very helpful. But her sermons bother me. That's what I especially wanted to talk with you about."

"She is very liberal, isn't she?" was Chan-Hie's response. "Some of the Christian Korean students say she's not a Christian at all. They go to Intervarsity meetings and stay away from the chapel."

"How do you feel about her yourself?"

"I appreciate her position. So much of Christianity is doctrinaire. I find it oppressive. It seems to negate and exclude all the traditional values of Korean culture. In seminary I began to find the freedom to think for myself. Some of my professors encouraged me to be proud of my Korean cultural and religious heritage. They introduced

19

me to some theologians who are rethinking Christian theology in terms of the Korean experience. It's heady stuff. I really don't know where it will lead. But I want to be free to explore it and to bring other Koreans into the exploration. Chaplain Levovsky has encouraged me."

"But can't you do all that without sacrificing belief in Jesus' divinity and in the universal power of his atonement?"

"I just don't know. Right now I feel freer and more honest to bracket those issues, to begin with the experience of the Korean people, and to see how Jesus is good news for them."

"How does that work out?" Thomas wanted to know.

"I don't have a lot of answers," Chan-Hie admitted. "But one thing that has meant a lot to me is to believe that God is like Jesus. That doesn't contradict a lot of our Korean religious beliefs, but it does help to sort them out. It also helps to sort out the beliefs Christian missionaries have brought to Korea. Sometimes Christian preachers there talk about God's tender and patient love. Then God seems very Christlike. Sometimes they talk about God's wrathful judgment in ways that I don't find revealed in Jesus at all. Anyway, Chaplain Levovsky suggested this to me, and I like it."

"I can see that up to a point," Thomas agreed. "If God is revealed in Jesus, then God must be like Jesus. But doesn't that have to mean that God is incarnate in him. If Jesus is just one man among others, why select him as the standard for judging what God is like?"

"You may well be right," said Chan-Hie. "I really have no objection to drawing that conclusion. But so many people who begin with Jesus' deity end up talking about things that don't make sense to me — about how he descended from heaven and why he gave up his equality with God. My point is only that I want to start somewhere else and see what happens. So far, I like what is happening."

"But doesn't that put Christian faith itself up for grabs? Maybe your explorations will lead you far away from Christian teaching. To me it sounds very dangerous indeed!"

"A good many of the Korean students here agree with you. I've already told you that. There's another group, though, who feel as I do. They're excited about what we're doing together. To us it *feels* very Christian. Indeed, it feels more Christian than just accepting what we're told to believe when it doesn't fit with our experience. But of course those feelings don't prove anything."

Thomas was intrigued. "What do you mean by saying 'it feels Christian'? I've always thought that whether something is Christian can be decided objectively by comparing it with the official teaching of the church. I doubt that feeling is a safe guide."

Chan-Hie agreed. "But I'm not sure orthodoxy is either. Some pretty horrible things have been done for the sake of doctrinal correctness."

"But at least," Thomas continued, "there has to be some center, and I don't see how for Christians that can be anything other than Jesus."

"I agree with you there!" Chan-Hie replied. "For me what has been attractive about Christianity has always been the gospel stories. I was taught to love Jesus in Sunday school, and the lessons took. That may be why I am so sure that God is like Jesus."

Thomas was not satisfied. "It seems to me that Christians are those who say Jesus was divine — human, of course, but not only that. He was completely unique, the one human being in whom God was incarnate. If not, isn't our continual preoccupation with this one human being inappropriate, even silly?"

"You've got me there," Chan-Hie admitted. "I know what I feel, that it's not so important how we think about Jesus as long as we follow him. But what you say makes sense, too. Why don't we talk with someone else about this. I've heard that Doris O'Connor of the religion department is a committed Christian and a fine scholar."

"But isn't she a Roman Catholic?" asked Thomas.

"I think so, but that doesn't mean she can't help us, does it?"

"I guess not," Thomas answered, a little embarrassed. "I'll call her right now."

• 5 •

Prof. O'Connor's Study— Thursday Afternoon

"WELL, GENTLEMEN, what can I do for you?" Prof. O'Connor asked, once the two young men were seated in her study. "You said you had a theological problem to discuss with me. I must warn you that I'm not a theologian. In my church few women are! My field is history of Christianity."

"Truthfully, your students speak so enthusiastically about your teaching that we thought you would be the ideal person to talk with. Thanks so much for seeing us so promptly." Chan-Hie began. "Tom and I got into a discussion of Christology, and we soon realized we needed help."

"My concern arose because of Chaplain Levovsky's views," Thomas interjected. "I've always thought that belief in the deity of Jesus is the heart of what it means to be a Christian, but she dismisses that as an obstacle to faith. It's hard for me to come to terms with that rejection."

"I haven't heard the chaplain much myself," Prof. O'Connor commented, "but she's known around here as a radical. I've often thought it's a good thing she's not ordained as a Catholic, although that's quite pointless, since if she were a Catholic she would not be ordained! Seriously, I mean that in the present climate of my church she would get into a lot of trouble. I'm really glad for the Protestant denominations! They give space for lots of practices and ideas that we don't seem able to tolerate — at least at present."

"Are you saying that the church should tolerate heresy, even on Christology?" Thomas challenged her.

"As a historian," she replied, "I've grown a little skeptical of hard and fast definitions of orthodoxy. Sometimes the orthodoxy of one generation becomes the heresy of the next. There was a scholar in ancient Alexandria, named Arius, who taught that the Logos, or Word, that became incarnate in Jesus was a supernatural creature, the first and greatest of all creatures. Back in the fourth century there was a whole generation of Christians who were taught that Arianism was orthodoxy. It was their missionaries who converted to Christianity many of the Germanic tribes who later overran much of the Western Roman Empire. It was hard to persuade them that the Christianity to which they had been converted was heretical, that they must believe that the Word incarnate in Jesus was truly God."

"I'm sure I would have trouble acknowledging that what I was brought up to believe was heresy," Thomas agreed.

"Also, when we study the councils at which the decisions were made, it isn't easy to be sure that faith and reason were always the causes of victory. A lot of what went on reads more like power politics."

Thomas had heard some of that before, but he hadn't been much affected by it. In his present mood he was more vulnerable. He commented almost sulkily, "You make it sound as though the creeds don't count for much."

Prof. O'Connor smiled: "Actually, I'm very glad Arianism lost out. I'm quite enthusiastic about the official teachings of the church about Christ."

"Why, then, make such a point of the vacillation between Arianism and what came to be orthodoxy?" Chan-Hie complained.

"I just mean to illustrate that Christological orthodoxy didn't fall from heaven. It is not taught by Jesus himself, and it can only with difficulty be read back into Paul. What is orthodox gets decided in very human struggles within the community of faith. I have a lot of confidence in that struggle. Over time bad ideas tend to lose out. But if you just determine to be orthodox, official teaching may change, and you'll have to scramble to change with it or end up a heretic."

"But hasn't Christology been pretty well set since the Council of Chalcedon in the fifth century?" Thomas persisted. "That's fifteen centuries; and the ancient creeds unite the Orthodox East, Roman Catholics, and mainstream Protestants! I've thought that was something to celebrate and cherish."

"You're right, Thomas. And I do want to be part of that great consensus. That's where I differ most from Chaplain Levovsky. She's a preacher who wants to talk to people today in their own language and context. I'm a historian who feels a part of a great community and who wants to make sense of what ancient people said and to appreciate it. But I'm glad she's doing what she's doing."

"I still don't understand you," Thomas fretted. "If there is a great consensus around the creeds, isn't the task of the preacher to explain the content of that consensus in today's language? It seems to me that Chaplain Levovsky wants to oppose the consensus. How can that be Christian?"

"I appreciate your persistence, Thomas. Maybe I do want to have my cake and eat it, too. But for me it's important to remember that even after the Council of

Chalcedon there were large groups of Christians who rejected what we call the orthodox Christology formulated there just because of their faith. One of these groups, the Nestorians, was for centuries an important factor in central Asia. Nestorian missionaries reached China and established churches there. And there were the Monophysites who dominated Egypt. They thought Chalcedon had given up the deity of Jesus!"

"But doesn't the fact that those heretical groups faded from history tell us something about the worth of their doctrines?" Thomas pressed her.

"I don't think so," Prof. O'Connor answered. "As I read history it was Muslim armies that reduced the Nestorians and the Monophysites to minor status. Somebody might argue that God raised up Mohammed to punish those Christians for their heresies, but that's not the way I see it. And we should not underestimate the power of Nestorian and Monophysite faith to stay alive even under the most adverse circumstances. There are still Nestorian churches, in Iraq, for example. And Coptic Christians, descendants of the Monophysites, are an important part of contemporary Egyptian life. Also, I think one reason we can celebrate the consensus is that we see Christianity through North Atlantic eyes. We forget that Ethiopia has been Christian longer than Western Europe and that its Christianity is Monophysite."

Chan-Hie liked what he was hearing. It supported his need for space to think what Christianity could be in modern Korea. He wanted to understand better what Prof. O'Connor was saying. "All the names you are throwing around are ones I've come across before, but frankly those Christological debates in the early church are a blur to me. Could you remind me what the issues were?"

Prof. O'Connor laughed. She sometimes spent several weeks in class trying to help her students understand,

and she knew from the exams that the blur was rarely dispelled. "I'll try," she said, "but don't expect too much in a few minutes!"

Chan-Hie also grinned. "I'll take what I can get. Maybe through repetition it will begin to sink in."

"Perhaps the easiest place to get a handle on those debates is in the first chapter of the Gospel of John. In the first verse we are told the Logos, or the Word, was in the beginning with God and that it was God. Later, in verse 14, it says the Logos became flesh and dwelt among us. That refers to Jesus, of course, the enfleshment or incarnation of the Logos."

"But what is the Logos, anyway?" Chan-Hie interrupted.

"We could say it is the same as the 'Son,' but then you might think directly of the historical Jesus, and that wouldn't do. Maybe the easiest way to get at it is to work backwards. The Logos is the aspect of the divine that was incarnate in Jesus. The church fathers agreed on that. But still they had two major debates about the Logos. First, how is the Logos related to the Father? Second, how was the Logos related to the human in Jesus?"

"Thanks," said Chan-Hie. "That distinction makes a lot of sense to me. I suppose the Council of Nicea dealt chiefly with the first and the Council of Chalcedon with the second."

"You get an A. You probably remember more of this than you thought! In any case, the major debate about the first question was whether the Logos was a creature or was truly God. The Arians said there could be only one God, the creator of all things, and that it demeaned God to suppose that God could take on finite, bodily form. They did not intend to belittle the Logos. On the contrary they held that God had created the Logos first, before creating the world, both as the agent of creation and as the agent of redemption. But still, the Logos was a creature. Athanasius and his followers objected that the Logos was truly God, not a creature. Since John distinguished the Logos from God as well as saying the Logos is God, they affirmed a distinction within the unity of God, between the Logos and the Father."

"That's why the doctrine of the Trinity became so important, I guess," said Chan-Hie, "once they brought in the Holy Spirit. If what is incarnate in Jesus is truly God and yet not identical with the Father, there has to be something like a distinction of persons within one substance. And that's what the Council of Nicea decided."

"It's a complicated story," Prof. O'Connor replied, "but you're on the right track. The debate about the relation of the Logos to the human in Jesus was somewhat different. After Arianism was finally overcome everyone agreed that the divine element in Jesus was truly God. But how could one conceive of a human being as containing God? I offer my students two basic images that sometimes help them see what was going on in the debates. Some Christians thought of the Logos as assuming humanity. Some thought that the Logos dwelt in a human being."

"Frankly," Chan-Hie commented, "I don't see much difference."

"It's hard to say whether there *has* to be much difference in the way those images work out, but in fact there was enough to create a lot of controversy. Those who thought of the Logos assuming humanity usually thought that what was most fundamental in Jesus was truly God and not human. God took on human form and characteristics, but Jesus was not in any full sense a human being. Chalcedon was responding to people who thought that way and who said that Jesus' nature was not human — only divine. These people said Jesus had only one nature — a divine one. In Greek that makes them Monophysites. Those people thought that to acknowledge a human nature in Jesus would undercut his deity."

"So Chalcedon's main point was not to affirm Jesus' deity but to affirm his humanity!" Thomas exclaimed.

"Yes, that's true, but of course it also affirmed, or reaffirmed, his deity. It had to satisfy those who thought that Nestorius had wrongly denied Jesus' deity."

"What was Nestorius's position?" Chan-Hie asked.

"Nestorius came from the side of those who thought of the Logos as dwelling in Jesus. They thought Jesus was truly a human being, human in every respect. The difference between Jesus and others was that God chose to dwell in Jesus fully. Thus Jesus had divine authority and was worthy of our worship as our Lord and Savior."

"What was wrong with that?" Chan-Hie asked.

"Frankly, I don't think anything was wrong. But much of the piety of the day expressed itself in ways that Nestorius didn't like. For example, people prayed to Mary as the Mother of God. Nestorius didn't like that language. God, who is eternal, cannot have a mother. Mary was the mother of the human being in whom God chose to dwell with fullness. That human being is Christ. So Nestorius taught the people to speak of Mary as the Mother of Christ. I would guess that you, as Protestants, are more comfortable with that, aren't you?"

She was right about that, and Thomas was trying to ransack his memory to recall what it was that he had been taught was wrong with Nestorius.

"But for people who thought of the Logos as assuming human form in Mary's womb, calling her Mother of God seemed proper. To them Nestorius's objections indicated that he was denying Jesus' deity. And long before the Council of Chalcedon they had him banished and his ideas rejected. In order to make sure that Nestorians were not allowed back in, Chalcedon stuck in a phrase about Mary the Mother of God even though otherwise it opposed those who had taken the lead in banishing Nestorius."

Thomas was both fascinated and troubled. Chalcedon no longer seemed like such a firm basis for one's faith. "So you're saying that the Chalcedonian Creed was a kind of compromise between the two ways of thinking, what you call the two images?"

"Yes, and the compromise worked for a good many people," Prof. O'Connor continued. It excluded on both sides those who had the most consistent ideas or images. It leaves us with a paradox or a mystery that has baffled the faithful. It has contributed to an idea of faith as acceptance on authority of what cannot be understood by the mind. I don't much like that. But still it has set some boundaries within which the discussion could go on."

"Then you do agree with me that it sets boundaries," said Thomas.

"Well, I agree with you that it has set boundaries," Prof. O'Connor replied. But I'm not saying that setting boundaries is altogether a good thing. In recent centuries a lot of Protestant thinkers have ignored those boundaries. When I read recent confessions and creeds of some of the more liberal Protestant denominations today, I'm not sure they are very close to Chalcedon. And I'm glad for all of that. I think ancient formulations are important, that we should pay a lot of attention to them. But I don't think any pronouncement settles issues forever."

Thomas felt a bit giddy. Every time he thought he could nail something down, it came loose again. He saw that she was taking much further the direction on which he was already embarked: holding herself to the traditional teaching but calling for openness for others to explore in whatever direction they were called. But surely she couldn't be open to all ideas whatsoever! Surely some proposals must be entirely beyond the pale. "But we do have to have some kind of boundaries, don't we? You're not going to accept Nazi Christianity as a legitimate exploration, are you?"

"That's a tough one," Prof. O'Connor admitted. "I hope that if I had been a Christian in Nazi Germany I would have resisted the Nazi influence. But I'm not sure that I really would have. And I'm also not sure that holding fast to Chalcedonian orthodoxy would have helped very much. Actually teaching that Jesus is truly God has led to a lot of anti-Jewish teaching, and anti-Jewish practice too. Most of the ideas of the Nazis about the Jews came right out of traditional Christian theology. It was only Hitler's "final solution" that went clearly beyond the teaching of the church against the Jews. The church had taught that the Jews should be restricted in all sorts of ways — punished for their stubborn refusal to accept Christian baptism. It was the duty of the state to make them suffer, but they should be kept alive until the last judgment. Hitler just exterminated them. Of course, Hitler's position is worse, but that doesn't make me proud of orthodox Christianity!"

Thomas was troubled, but he had to push on. "Does that mean that you don't set any boundaries at all?"

"In spite of all the evil that has been done by the church, I'm still disposed to trust the community of faithful over the long haul. That means that we should let people think creatively and freely. Eventually the bad ideas will be exposed. Today we're realizing that we must change those Christian teachings that led to the Holocaust. We're searching around in our heritage for other ways of understanding what it means to be Christian, ways that don't imply that the Jews are Christ-killers and that they have lost their covenant with God by rejecting Jesus. If everyone had been held tightly to orthodoxy during the past centuries, we might not find much to draw on. I'm disposed to let time decide."

Thomas could not accept that. He needed criteria now. "But surely today there are theologies you reject and reject strongly."

"Indeed, Thomas. But to reject them and to want them silenced by church authority are two quite different matters. I want to be free to argue my case against them vigorously. But I want them to be free to talk back. I may even have to change my mind. Ideas that I now object to strongly may prove convincing to our grandchildren. They may be just the ideas our descendants will need in order to deal with their new situation. Remember, the ideas of the early prophets were rejected in their time, but later they provided the basis for the Jewish people to rebuild their faith after the Babylonian captivity."

Thomas found it strange that what he had been taught were Protestant views were coming to him from a Roman Catholic. "But what's the point of church doctrine if everything is always up for grabs?"

"That's a very reasonable response to my one-sided emphasis, isn't it?" Prof. O'Connor answered. "I'm probably reacting too strongly against the new authoritarianism of the Vatican. I owe my own enthusiasm for the church to the vitality and freedom I felt in the late sixties in the aftermath of the Second Vatican Council, when Pope John XXIII threw the windows of the church open to the best thought of the modern world. But Vatican II is a good example of the value of official church teaching. It now functions to restrain the reactionaries somewhat. I certainly don't want to knock that!"

"But even Vatican II didn't raise questions about the Christological creeds," Chan-Hie pointed out. "How can you as a Catholic be open to ideas that oppose those."

"We Catholics have always had more doctrinal freedom than you Protestants have recognized," Prof. O'Connor protested laughingly. "We see that it is the whole church that corporately grows in the understanding of the truth. Wherever we find the whole church has expressed its shared understanding, we treat what is said as authoritative. As Thomas pointed out, the Christological creeds come close to an ecumenical consensus. That gives them a lot of authority.

"After the Protestant Reformation and the subsequent Roman Catholic Council at Trent, Catholics tended to narrow their view of the church to just the Roman Catholic church and leave it to the pope to tell them what the consensus is. That was not the true Catholic spirit. John XXIII threw open the windows. We recognized that there are lots of good Christians whose thinking had not had to kowtow to Vatican authority, that we could learn from them. Some of the most interesting work on Christology has gone back behind the creeds to the New Testament. What it finds there may or may not fit with the later creeds. Maybe we should stick with the creeds. Maybe we should go back to the New Testament and follow the leads we get there wherever they take us. Who can say? I want enough freedom for both to be tried by believing Christians. Generations can discuss and live with the results. I trust that process. Somehow God works through it. New consensus will emerge out of open discussion. Drawing boundaries and enforcing silence only slows the process."

For the first time Thomas began to feel some positive excitement about this different way of thinking of Christian doctrine. But it was also disturbing — frightening really. It meant living without any solid ground under your feet. The image he had was of finding himself in a stream, not knowing where it was taking him. In that stream one could no longer settle disputes by appeal to orthodoxy. The question would always be one of the merits of every view. But who could decide that? Wouldn't the fragmentation and individualism of Protestantism just get worse? Maybe the Catholics had a sense of the church that could hold them together. But it had always been hard for Protestants who disagreed about doctrine to work and worship together very long.

Chan-Hie was talking. "I really like that. For me Jesus is at the center of my faith, but I haven't wanted to commit myself to any doctrine about him. I like the idea of openness to lots of teachings, testing them practically in the ongoing life of the church."

Thomas yielded somewhat. "I guess I may be too insistent that a Christian has to make central some traditional doctrine about Jesus. If Jesus himself is central for people, I suppose they should be free to consider various doctrines about him. But I don't see how one can avoid holding that there was something special about his relation to God. Even with all the openness it seems to me Chaplain Levovsky goes too far."

"Maybe you should talk with her again," Prof. O'Connor suggested. "Maybe she really doesn't deny that there was something special about Jesus' relation to God. You noticed that a lot of what *I* said was in reaction to the tightening of the reigns in my own church. I seem to see something like that in Protestant denominations, too. I suspect that she is reacting against what still seems to her to be the mumbo-jumbo of orthodoxy. When she's not feeling pressured to use that language, she'll probably talk more positively about Jesus."

That made sense to Thomas, and he agreed to talk with the chaplain again. Chan-Hie wanted to join him. "You've been more than generous with your time, Prof. O'Connor," he said. "I can see why your students appreciate your teaching so much. Thanks a lot."

• 6 •

Chaplain's Office —
Friday Morning

CHAPLAIN LEVOVSKY GREETED THE YOUNG MEN WARMLY. She was fortunate in her interns this year. They were both serious, hardworking, and able to establish rapport with at least some of the students. But she was worried, too. She had always been outspoken, and that meant she "rocked the boat" both at the university and in her denomination. She knew she was appointed university chaplain partly because she was a woman. The university liked the idea of a woman chaplain whereas most congregations still resisted women pastors, at least as senior pastors. A couple of men who had wanted the job were envious and resented what they considered to be reverse discrimination. There were also conservatives in the denomination who would like to embarrass her. Politically she had good reason to be careful. She had not been careful with Thomas, and she had upset him. Intentionally or not, he might make trouble for her. When he had asked for another appointment, she had hastened to arrange it. She wondered why Chan-Hie had come. She couldn't believe that he shared Thomas's concerns.

"Did you want to continue the inquisition?" she asked, smiling, but at once regretting the tone of her question.

"Not exactly," answered Thomas. "But I do want to try to understand your theology better. I've been talking with Chan-Hie, and we both had a conversation with Prof. O'Connor. I think I may be more able to understand what you're saying now than I was on Tuesday. And Chan-Hie got interested, too. I hope you don't mind."

The chaplain was somewhat reassured. The young men seemed to be genuinely seeking. She remembered delegations of conservative students in the past whose tack had been quite different. This seemed like a positive challenge. If only she could let go of her defensiveness! "I don't mind at all. Really I appreciate your interest. I know I'm not much of a theologian, but I do have strong convictions, and I hope I can explain them sensibly. Anyway, I can try."

"I was so upset last time we talked by your attack on Jesus' deity that I didn't even ask you what you do think of Jesus. I know Jesus is important to you, because you bring him into your sermons a lot. I know you think he was human, but if that were all I don't suppose you would talk about him much. Everybody else is human too. Is there anything special about Jesus for you?"

Chan-Hie broke in. "Tom has pushed me in the same way. He wants me to say why Jesus is so important to me. He thinks that has to mean that I believe that Jesus is divine. I don't know. That's why I came along to hear what you have to say."

"I'm glad you came, Chan-Hie. And you're right, of course, Thomas. I do think Jesus was quite special. I did say something about that on Tuesday, but it wasn't what you were looking for then. The Spirit I serve was released to new effectiveness in history because of Jesus. That makes Jesus special. But you're asking about Jesus himself rather than about the effects of his ministry on others. I haven't thought as much about that. But I do see the Holy Spirit present and at work in him. Since the Holy Spirit is God, I can say God was incarnate in Jesus. I really like incarnational language."

The language was familiar, but the context was sufficiently different that Thomas did not trust it. "But would you say that God is incarnate in everyone else, too?"

Chaplain Levovsky wondered how she should answer that. It was the old question about whether Jesus differs from us in degree or in kind. She knew she was against a difference in kind and she resolved to speak frankly. "Yes, or at least in some others. There are some people and communities in which I have a hard time finding any trace of the Spirit I serve. I think God is specially present among those who have faith and try to be open to the working of grace. I think of the church as the community in which the Spirit lives with particular fullness. I don't want to say that Jesus was fundamentally different. Because of Jesus, we can also be daughters and sons of God as he was God's son."

"If you're saying that Jesus was the first in whom God was incarnate and that this incarnation has extended to those who believe in him, I could at least recognize that as a traditional way of thinking." Thomas was wondering aloud. He was really trying now to connect her liberal ideas with classical ones. This was a new kind of undertaking for him.

"Thanks, I appreciate your help," the chaplain answered, "and I do find that image meaningful, but I can't quite say that. I'm sure the Spirit was at work in the world before Jesus. The Hebrew Scripture speaks of it. And I'm sure God is present in other religions as well. I simply won't tie God down just to please the orthodox."

Her hostility to the rigidities of orthodoxy had gotten

the best of her again. She knew there were other moves she could make, fully supported by Scripture and tradition, that would render her position more acceptable to conservatives. But she was impatient with that theological game. Maybe it kept peace within the church, she thought, but one always ended up with the sort of language that had so alienated her parents. Why not just say what she believed in contemporary ways?

"You confuse me, Chaplain," Thomas admitted. "Part of the time it sounds as though Jesus were really very special for you, but then you deny it."

"Probably the truth is that I'm confused, too. Jesus does seem very special to me. God seems to me especially real and present in him. But I get upset when people want to say *only* in Jesus. To me it seems that over thousands of years millions of people have found God in other persons as well. I've read a little about Confucius and Gautama Buddha and Lao Tze, and I can see why people have found God in them, too. I don't want to diminish them in order to exalt Jesus. So I draw back from the kinds of statements you might find reassuring."

"I really appreciate that," was Chan-Hie's response. Some Koreans are beginning to say that the missionaries did not bring God to Korea. God had been there all along. The missionaries often made us ashamed of Shamanism, Confucianism, and Buddhism. From what they said, it sounded as though all our ancestors were damned! I've never believed that. My Buddhist grandmother was a fine woman. She would go with the family to church. Her husband and her children kept hoping she would convert, but she refused to be baptized and died a Buddhist. I rather respected her for it. I'm sure God respected her too."

"The way you're both talking makes me think you don't believe in missions at all," Thomas exploded. "You seem to think all religions are equally good. There are many ways to salvation. We should all just mind our own business. This relativism is just what I feared would happen if the orthodox creeds are abandoned!"

Chan-Hie responded quickly. "Thomas, I didn't say that. It's true that we tend to be critical of the missionaries these days. But that's partly in reaction to having admired them so much and followed them so blindly. They may not be so much to blame for having belittled Korean culture. They didn't know much about it. But we are at fault if they make us ashamed of it. We all thank God for the missionaries even when we cut them down to size as fallible human beings. They brought us the knowledge of Jesus that is so important to me."

Chaplain Levovsky replied also. "I do support missions. We've taken up special collections for missions twice since you've been here, I think. We should share what we know and our goods as well. But in our denomination the main effort of Western missions today is not the conversion of Muslims, Hindus, and Buddhists. It is serving the common people, sometimes in alliance with Muslims, Hindus, and Buddhists. Of course, we still establish congregations and are happy to accept new members. In some countries in Africa our churches are growing rapidly while they are declining here in the United States. But we don't consider getting new members the main thing. For us, to serve Christ is just as much to feed the hungry, to teach people to read, and to help them in their struggle for justice, as it is to baptize them."

Thomas knew that most of the evangelism on the mission field was left to indigenous leadership. The role of missionaries had changed. But still he had thought of missions primarily as bringing people to Christ. The idea of missions as working *with* other religions did not have the right ring. Every time he felt that he could extend the hand of Christian fellowship a little further, more was demanded of him. He could see why real conservatives were sure it was better to hold the lines tight. He felt himself on a slippery slope. This was all he could take today.

Chan-Hie was enjoying the conversation, but when he saw that Thomas was restless, he suggested that it was time to go. Chaplain Levovsky was reluctant to end like that. "Before you go," she suggested, "could we pray together?" Of course they agreed. They prayed silently for awhile. Then Chaplain Levovsky prayed aloud:

"Spirit of love, draw us together in true community. Spirit of life, enliven us in your service. Spirit of truth, enlighten our minds and lead us into wisdom. Amen."

"I do hope you'll come to talk again," she said. "Next time let's talk about your ideas instead of mine."

• 7 •

At Home — Friday Evening

Mary was too excited to pay much attention to Thomas's dejection when he arrived home. "While you were out the Schmidts called. You know, Judy and Mike. They are in town and asked if they could come by to see us. Of course, I invited them to dinner. You know how much I've enjoyed Judy — and Mike, too, for that matter. It will be fun to hear what's been going on at the seminary since we've been away."

Thomas's reactions were mixed. He felt the need to be alone, to try to come to terms with the confusion and distress he was experiencing. But he could also see the advantage of an evening of conversation with friends. Maybe the contact with familiar faces and familiar ideas could restore his assurance. Both of the Schmidts were students, and good students at that. Maybe they would help him reach some decision about what to do. At any rate the die was cast. "Great!" he said, trying to sound enthusiastic.

As always, Mary served a delicious dinner with style. She asked about their friends, and the Schmidts enjoyed telling stories about recent events, especially about some of the more eccentric professors. Toward the end of dinner

Judy mentioned something about her class in Christology. That gave an opening for Thomas.

"That's a topic I've been quite concerned about lately, Judy. I wish I had had the course."

"Well," Judy laughed, "I'm hardly an expert after six weeks of classes, but I'll be glad to share whatever I can. What's the problem?"

"The problem is that my chaplain supervisor doesn't believe any of the things I believe about Jesus." Thomas knew he exaggerated, but at the moment that was how it seemed. "If she's right, I'm on quite the wrong course. If I'm right, she's hardly a Christian at all — certainly not a suitable supervisor for seminarians."

"Wow! That's a *real* problem," Judy replied, some-what sobered. "I'm not sure I can help with that, but let's talk about it. Who *is* your supervisor, and what does he believe?"

"Chaplain Levovsky, and she's a woman, and a very fine woman I might add. If I didn't think so highly of her I wouldn't be bothered so by her ideas. When it gets right down to it, she thinks Jesus was a man like other men. She sees God in him and gives him credit for the emergence of the church. But she thinks other communities have found God in other people. There's no need to convert Muslims and Hindus. We should work with them in meeting social needs."

"I can see that she's pretty far on the liberal side," Judy replied. "But you know, I'm sympathetic with some of it. I haven't thought much about Muslims and Hindus, but I have been thinking a lot about women. Did you know that I've been in a women's support group? That's been pretty disturbing too! Some of the members claim that women can't be saved by a male savior, that looking to a man for salvation just confirms unhealthy dependence on men. If we say that to be Christian is to believe that Jesus is the only savior, some of my friends reply that they can't be Christian any longer.

"But I don't see any choice," Thomas exploded. "Even Chaplain Levovsky wouldn't say that a *Christian* has some other savior than Jesus."

"It's a real problem, I grant you. Some try to get around it by saying that Jesus had strong feminine traits, that he was androgynous. Others say that the relation to him has nothing to do with his gender. Still others suggest that we should look not so much to Jesus the man, but to the Christ-event that includes men and women."

"But where do you come down yourself?" Mary broke in. She was even more shocked than Thomas, but she had a deep confidence in Judy.

"Well," said Judy, "really I haven't come down. I guess the idea I've liked the best is an emphasis on the future. God came to us in a man. That's true. But that man pointed ahead to what was to come. The *basileia theou*. We translate that 'the Kingdom of God,' and that sounds very masculine indeed. But a *basileia* does not have to have a king. The word itself is feminine, and I think that as we envision what the *basileia* is to be, the dominance of males and male values ceases."

"But I don't see how the fact that *basileia* is a feminine noun has much to do with whether women can be saved by Jesus," Thomas was impatient to return to this issue.

"To me it does seem related," Judy answered. "We have to consider what salvation really is. A lot of theology today points to the future as the time of salvation. Jesus announced salvation and foreshadowed it, for example, in his table fellowship with all kinds of people. In that way he mediates salvation to us. He gives us assurance. But to believe this is not to depend on a man to save us. We depend on God to bring the *basileia*. When I think in those ways it doesn't matter that Jesus was a male. What does matter is whether the promised salvation will meet the needs of women as well as men."

"That does make sense, I guess," said Thomas, a little reluctantly, "though that's not the way I've thought of it. I think of Jesus' atonement on the cross as that which saves all who by faith identify with his dying and rising. I guess that's just what bothers the feminists — identifying with a male savior. But I don't see how that relates to finding God in more than one person."

"Well, if we need figures who foreshadow the final salvation, it seems much better to us women if some of them are women. Jesus may have an extra special place. I for one don't object to that. But I also see a foreshadowing of the *basileia* in Ruth, in Esther, in Mary Magdalene, in Catherine of Siena, in Sojourner Truth, and in Mother Teresa. In other words, I see God incarnate in both women and men, and now I am inclined to minimize the differences between Jesus and these incarnations instead of maximizing them as I once did."

"Has your work in the Christology course tied in with this at all?" Mary asked. She was bewildered but not entirely lost. She had read a little feminist theology and felt mildly sympathetic. But it had never occurred to her that feminists would want to downplay Jesus just because he was a man!

"Yes, Mary, somewhat, although we haven't gotten to any feminist theologians yet. I think one or two will be tacked on at the end. We have been exposed to theologians of hope, and I've already told you that I think the emphasis on the future helps. In addition I've found in Donald Baillie a way to think about God's incarnation in Jesus that doesn't separate Jesus so much from others."

"You're referring to *God Was in Christ*, aren't you?" asked Thomas. I read that a couple of years ago, and it didn't seem particularly important then. But these last few days I've found myself wondering whether I should re-read it."

"I do recommend it," Judy replied. "Baillie makes sense of something that perplexed me for a long time, long before I became a feminist. How can one person be both fully God and fully human? I could make the statement that he was, but I didn't really know what I was saying. After reading Baillie I saw that the problem was that I thought of deity and humanity as external to one another. Baillie enabled me to see that the more fully God is in us — we call that grace — the more genuinely human we are."

"I like that," said Mary quietly. "Jesus was fully human *because* he was fully divine. But that makes Jesus very different from the rest of us, even the saintly women of whom you spoke."

"Probably Baillie would agree with you," Judy acknowledged. "He seems to want to see incarnation as like grace, but still different, although he doesn't explain how. But I see God's incarnation in grace as the only incarnation there is. It may have been more complete in Jesus than in anyone else. I don't know. But it can't be different in kind. If God is present in human beings, God is incarnate to some degree, and in some special people that incarnation becomes peculiarly clear. For now, I'm satisfied with that."

Thomas was not satisfied with that, but he was bothered now by something else. Chaplain Levovsky had talked so easily of God being present in people. Judy did, too, and apparently Mary found that easy to accept. But he didn't. How could God be *in* something. He thought of God's presence as personal encounter. Of course, he did affirm God's incarnation in Jesus. But that was utterly supernatural, utterly unique, a complete mystery! One was not supposed to understand it. In Jesus the impossible happened. That's what made all the difference.

Baillie at least recognized the problem, Thomas remembered. Baillie emphasized that what he said was
paradoxical. But Thomas wasn't accustomed to thinking
of God's grace as being God internal to people. For him
God's grace is God's forgiveness of our sins, the gift of
life and new life. It might be that Baillie is right, that the
more we receive from God the more human we are, but
for Thomas that was a far cry from incarnation. In grace
God gives things to us and forgives us. In incarnation,
God becomes a human being.

"As you talk about Baillie," he said at last, "it makes
him sound like a mystic, as if God were found within us,
or as if God's being merged with ours. I wasn't struck by
that when I read him. I thought he was more orthodox
than that."

"You're right. Maybe my interpretation is more mystical than he intends. But I think if it's mystical, it's a biblical
mysticism. It's not a merging of ourselves into the divine
or a denial of the ultimate difference between God and
creatures. It's just that the supreme gift of grace is God's
own presence within us, liberating, empowering, and di-
recting us. I can't think of that as an external force. I find it
working in me. It's part of my experience. And, as Baillie
says, the more effective it is in shaping my life, the more
fully I'm human, that is, the freer, stronger, more fulfilled
and effective I am as a human being."

Thomas could remember Paul's language about Christ
and the Holy Spirit as within us making us free and
strengthening us. He had to admit there was biblical justification for *that* kind of mysticism. Indeed, he wished he
felt the Spirit at work in him as Judy seemed to feel it in
her. But the idea of something other than himself being
within him still didn't make much sense. "I wish I could
experience something like that," he said, "but even if I did
I wouldn't understand how God could be in me!"

"I have trouble with that, too." Mike spoke up for the first time. "It's hard for me to think of anything in me except myself. I think of God as present to me, not present in me. But have you noticed that it's usually the women who think of God present in them and the men who think more of encountering God as one who comes to them from beyond?"

"No, Mike, I hadn't connected the difference with gender," Thomas admitted.

"It was Prof. Matsumoto who pointed this out to me. He also pointed out that it's something of an East-West distinction, too. In the East, at least in China, Korea, and Japan, people think of things or events as made up of their relations to everything else. The Buddhists talk about "dependent origination." An event or an experience is just the coming together of other things. There isn't any boundary separating its inside from its outside."

"Sorry," Thomas interrupted him. "This is coming too fast for me. But it sounds important. What is Prof. Matsumoto saying?"

"I'm not sure I fully understand, Tom, but I did take a course from him on Hinduism and Buddhism, and that helped, the Buddhist part especially. Just think about your experience right now. Then think about what I'm saying. Is it inside or outside your experience."

"Well," Thomas answered hesitantly, "I guess that distinction doesn't work, does it. Of course, what I hear and understand is part of my experience. But since you are the source, it is certainly coming to me from outside. So it's both inside and outside — or neither. Is that the Buddhist point?"

"That's part of what I've gotten out of it, at any rate. If you follow that line of thought through, you'll see that if you're related to God at all, then God is both outside and inside your experience — or neither — in the same way.

The God who is in your experience is also much more than your experience. More traditionally we've talked about God being both immanent and transcendent."

"Okay, I accept that." Thomas agreed. "But my experience isn't me. I am the one to whom the experiences happen or the one who possesses the experiences. I've had other experiences in the past, and I'll have more in the future. Maybe God is in the experiences in the way you say, but that doesn't put God inside of me."

"That's a tough one," Mike agreed. "I raised the same point with Prof. Matsumoto. He just said: That's the problem with you Westerners. That left me puzzled and a bit angry. I started to say that was Christian teaching. But then he's a Christian, too, and I knew he would ask me where it was stated in the Bible that the self is separate and distinct from the experiences. I shut up and listened."

"And what do you think about it now?" Thomas asked.

"The longer I live with that way of thinking the more sense it makes to me."

"Well, offhand," Thomas complained, "it doesn't make that much sense to me. When I decide to do something, it's not just an experience that decides. My decision leads to changes in experience."

"You're right, Tom, and Prof. Matsumoto acknowledged that Eastern thought hasn't dealt very well with deciding. In fact, he says that it was writings about decision and personal ethical responsibility that led him to Christ. But does it help any to think of the 'I' who decides as outside of experience? I've come to think of my 'self' as one aspect of the experience, affecting all the rest, as you say, but also affected by all the rest."

Mary broke in. "This is way beyond me. I do think of God as in me. Indeed, I feel that way about my relations with other people too. And maybe that *is* because I'm a woman. I don't know. But what Buddhism has to do with it I don't understand."

Judy saw that Mary was tired and that if they got any deeper into these mysteries, she might really get upset. Considering that she was the only one of the group who was not studying theology, she held her own very well in these discussions. But enough was enough. "It's getting late. We really must be going. We have a big day tomorrow, and I know you are busy, too. Dinner was delicious. You're a great cook, Mary!"

"Yes, indeed,"agreed Mike sincerely. "And it's been a long time since I've enjoyed a theological discussion so much. Good luck with Chaplain Levovsky!"

• 8 •

Thomas Alone in His Study — Saturday Morning

THOMAS HAD NOT SLEPT WELL after the conversation with Judy and Mike. He didn't know whether he was more upset or excited. So many things that used to be clear were confused! So many settled planks in his belief system had come loose! But at the same time it seemed that new doors were opening up. He was certainly not ready to write the seminary saying that Chaplain Levovsky was not a suitable chaplain supervisor. But he was not ready to decide not to write either. He had to sort things out.

Thomas had found that when he was confused, he needed to sit with paper and pen and at least identify in writing what he was confused about. He wrote down two headings and then made notes on each. Several pages went into the trash basket. But after a couple of hours he had an outline like the one on the following page.

Tom felt better after he had gotten all this out on paper. He knew there were lots more questions, and he knew that he didn't have the answers. But he also knew that he was shifting. The Pauline passages about Christ and the Holy Spirit being "in" the believer were taking on a

I. The boundaries of legitimate Christian
   thinking—the problem of heresy.
   A. Are there established doctrines all
      Christians should accept?
   B. If so, what are they?
   C. If not, how do Christians decide what to
      believe?
      - Bible, creeds, tradition central but not
        wholly decisive.
      - Maybe Jesus himself is crucial.
      - What makes sense to us—how important is
        this? Can we believe what does not make
        sense to us? Should we?
II. What do I think about Jesus Christ?
   A. How I think of God's presence is crucial
      here.
      - If God is present to human beings but not
        in them, then God's incarnation in Jesus
        was wholly unique.
      - If God is present in others as well, then
        God's incarnation in Jesus may not be so
        very different. (I must re-read Baillie.)
   B. If God is present in people other than Jesus,
      is this just in Christians or is it in others
      as well?
      - If only in Christians, then Jesus'
        uniqueness remains very important. (Paul
        connects the Spirit to belief in Jesus'
        Lordship.)
      - If in everyone, then Christianity seems to
        be only one expression of God's saving
        work. (John says the Word enlightened
        everyone who came into the world.)
   C. In what way is Jesus savior?
      - Did he atone for the sins of all on the
        cross? (Or, all who were predestined to
        be saved?)
      - Did he preach the coming of a basileia in
        which God's will would be done?
      - Did he initiate a community in which God's
        Spirit is effective?
      - If all the above, how are they related?

real meaning for him. He wasn't willing to let that go. He would follow where that led, even if it led part of the way that Prof. O'Connor and Chaplain Levovsky went. Part of that *was* genuinely Christian. Even if it reduced the difference between Jesus and believers, Thomas decided, he could live with that, too. After all Paul did talk about our becoming sons and daughters of God through faith in the one Son of God.

Paul, however, definitely did *not* say that Jesus provides just one way of salvation alongside others. He didn't say, "Let the Ephesians go on worshiping Diana; she'll do just as well as Jesus." No! Paul had no doubt about the boundaries. And Thomas would stay with Paul.

But then what about Chan-Hie's Buddhist grand-mother? Did God damn her for her stubborn refusal to accept Christian baptism? Thomas did not feel comfortable saying that — at least not to Chan-Hie. But wasn't there something wrong with holding theological doctrines and then refusing to draw the consistent conclusions in particular cases?

Thomas realized that he had long been uncomfortable about the implications of his theology in one area. In college he had attended a two-day conference on the Holocaust. He had become aware for the first time of how deeply Christians, and even official church teaching, especially about Jesus, had contributed to the Holocaust. The idea that all Jews deserved punishment because some long ago had called for Jesus' crucifixion was certainly cruel and unjust! The conversation with Prof. O'Connor had brought those painful memories back. He could sympathize with the commitment of some of the Jews to keep the Jewish people alive at all costs and to fight off all efforts at Christian conversion. He accepted the comments of some Christians that the church has forfeited the right to try to convert Jews. He was glad to hear that his denomination did not support missions to Jews. But he gave up trying to make sense of this theologically. Vaguely he thought that since Jews are a chosen people, God will work things out for them and we Christians can leave this matter to God.

But now the challenge was much wider. The implication seemed to be to leave everyone alone — and everything to God. That sounded wrong — dead wrong.

He couldn't put the matter aside this time. He had to come to terms with it. Could people find salvation through other religions — Buddhism, for example? How could he decide? He knew so little about it. Then it occurred to him that there was a Fellowship of Buddhist Students that met once a week on campus — in the chapel as a matter of fact. Of course, Chaplain Levovsky would see nothing wrong with that! Maybe he could attend a meeting and make the acquaintance of some of the Buddhists. Perhaps he would even win some of them to Christ! In any case, learning something about them would help him to think about the question.

• 9 •

A Meeting of the Buddhist Fellowship — Monday Evening

A DOZEN STUDENTS WERE SEATED IN A CIRCLE with a couple of empty chairs. One of the students got up to meet Thomas as he came to the door. "I'm Bill Putnam, the one you called. I've told the others that you were coming. We appreciate your interest in visiting our group. The student interns in the past have pretty much ignored us."

"Thanks, Bill. But I'm afraid I'm not coming in my official capacity. I'm coming more out of my own need to understand something about Buddhism."

"All the better," said Bill. "But none of us are scholars. Prof. Wilson knows a lot more about Buddhism than any of us will ever know. But maybe getting to know some Buddhists will supplement your study. Anyway, we're glad you're here. Is there anything in particular we can do to help you?"

Thomas was embarrassed. He had meant to slip into the back of a room where Buddhists were worshipping just to get some sense of what was going on. "I didn't mean to interrupt. I wish you would just go ahead with your services and let me sit here with you."

"I'm afraid we don't have what you could call a service," Alice Kaufman spoke up. "Before you came we were meditating for about an hour. But we don't have a teacher, and we come from different traditions; so even that is awfully loose. After meditating we like to sit and talk about our lives as Buddhists at a Christian university. Since you've come, we would like to talk about whatever would interest you."

Something had been bothering Thomas without his being clear what it was. Suddenly he realized that, without thinking about it consciously, he had been expecting that Buddhists would be Asians. But in this group only two looked Asian. These young people were not Buddhists just because they had been brought up to be Buddhists! Living in a predominantly Christian culture, they had *chosen* to be Buddhists. Why? "Thanks," he said. "I guess what would help me most would be to hear you talk about why you are Buddhists, what it means to you."

"No two of us would answer that in the same way," Alice replied, "but I, too, think it would be the best way to get acquainted. I'll speak for myself, and then some of the others can talk.

"I grew up in a very secular home. My father was a secular Jew and my mother called herself a Protestant but never showed any signs of interest in going to church or sending me there. They seemed content to enjoy what are called the good things of life, and we always had plenty of them. They were very good to me. I had what's called a happy childhood, but still I wasn't quite satisfied. Looking back I would say things were too flat, too superficial. I was hungry for more depth.

"I had heard people talk about mysticism, sometimes positively and sometimes contemptuously. It sounded like 'depth.' I decided to try to learn about it. I read some Christian mystics such as Brother Lawrence, Evelyn Underhill, and Thomas Merton. I liked what I read, and I thought I might become a Christian.

"I visited some churches during that period, a synagogue, too. My parents had no objection. But I couldn't make any connection between what I found there and what had appealed to me in my reading. I even talked with a priest once and also a rabbi. But they both discouraged my mystical interests. They thought what I needed was to be involved in their youth programs. But those seemed as flat to me as my homelife.

"It was through Merton that I got acquainted with the writings of the Buddhist missionary to this country, D. T. Suzuki. That was when I really came alive. I read everything I could find by him. I'm not saying I understood him, just that he spoke to me. I decided I was a Buddhist. I wanted to be saved in the Buddhist sense: to attain enlightenment. But I never met another Buddhist until I came here to the university. It has been great to find others who are really concerned with personal religious experience and can help me learn to meditate. I'm a long, long way from experiencing enlightenment, but meditation has come to mean a great deal to me. I know something genuine happens, something that's quite strange to my parents and their friends — and to the Christians I know, too."

I'm afraid I don't really know what you're saying," Thomas admitted. "I know something about mysticism, of course, at least from reading about it. Are you saying that Suzuki pointed you to the mystical experience better than Merton did?"

"I don't know whether the Buddhist experience is mystical or not," Alice answered. "In one sense it seems so very ordinary and secular. It's just realizing what's really going on, letting things be what they are, not imposing our ideas and expectations on them, not interpreting them in terms of our desires and fears, just letting go of everything we've clung to. Of course, I haven't accomplished all that. But in bits and pieces I have come to feel free and more alive, more present. The world seems fresher and more zestful. So I get a sense of what full enlightenment would be, and meanwhile I'm grateful for the changes that are taking place in me."

Thomas did not know what to say. He was glad Bill spoke up.

"I guess I should go next. My story is different. I was brought up in the church, a quite conservative church. There was a lot of talk about the danger of eternal damnation and how we are saved by the blood of Jesus. We were even encouraged to give a lot of money to save the souls of the heathen. It wasn't at all what Alice calls 'flat.' People were excited and intense and deeply committed.

"Since it was the only world I knew, I believed everything I was told. But one day I met one of those 'heathen.' My neighbors had travelled in India, and a Hindu family who had befriended them there came to spend a week with them. When my neighbors saw me looking on curiously, they invited me to come over to meet the visitors. I was twelve at the time, and I was fascinated by the difference in dress, manners, and accent. I spent as much time with them as I could. I had never met such gracious, cultivated, and genuinely devout people.

"I could not fit that experience with what I heard in church, and I'm afraid I became a rebel. My parents forced me to go to Sunday school, church, and youth group. But all I did was cut up and ask embarrassing questions. The church was relatively tolerant of adolescent rebellion, but mine went too far. No one admitted it, but they were all glad when my parents gave up and let me stop going.

"Meanwhile I had begun to read about India and especially about Indian religion. It sounded so much more profound and true than what I had heard in church. It was also much more tolerant. They could accept Jesus as an avatar or a Boddhisattva, a manifestation of the divine, and they did not deny that people could find salvation through faith in him. That seemed so much better than the church's teaching that God sends everyone to hell who doesn't believe as it teaches.

"There were other things I liked, too. They were concerned for other animals, not only human beings. I've always been horrified by the way we raise and butcher animals. But in Christian circles people made fun of me for being so sentimental. God gave us animals to kill and eat, I was told. They have no souls. In the literature of India I found a deep compassion for all sentient beings. I became a vegetarian and stood my ground against Christian ridicule. Finally, I announced that I was a Buddhist, not because the differences between Hinduism and Buddhism mattered to me. I didn't understand them. But the stories of the life and teachings of the Buddha moved me deeply. He was so selfless, so serene, so profound, and he generated such peace among those with whom he spoke.

"That really shocked my parents and their friends. They preferred that I be a rebel and renegade. I think they would have been happier if I had become a drug addict than a well-behaved, conscientious Buddhist. I'm afraid their reaction didn't do much to improve my image of Christianity.

"But let me hasten to say I don't feel so negative any longer. If all Christians were like Chaplain Levovsky, I would see Christianity as a wonderful religion. What a great woman! She even meditates with us sometimes. But it's your time to tell us about yourself. How did you come to your Christian faith, and what do you believe as a Christian? Do you think God is going to throw us all into everlasting torment because we are Buddhists?"

Thomas suddenly felt embarrassed that he had thought he might be able to bring some of these Buddhists to Christ. What could he say? Warn them that indeed they must turn to Christ to escape hellfire? No, that would only confirm their worst suspicions of Christianity. Anyway, faced with the spiritual journeys of Alice and Bill, he certainly could not condemn them. Would God be less understanding than he? "No, of course not," he murmured. He grew very uncomfortable. He really didn't feel like telling his story. What was there to tell? He had accepted what he was told as a child, deeply internalized it, and sincerely tried to live by it. He had never really searched, not until now. What kind of a testimony to Christ would it be to tell them that? The room was feeling very warm. "Thanks very much for sharing with me," he muttered. "I've got to go."

Outside and alone he could not remember ever being so miserable. He had been invited to give his Christian witness, and he had run away instead. But worse, he had decided he had no witness to give! He did not even know whether he was a believer. "Maybe *all* this stuff about Jesus is just hocum," he thought wretchedly. "Maybe even Chaplain Levovsky puts too much stock in it." For the first time in his twenty-four years Thomas was doubting, really doubting. "There may not be any literal hell as a separate place," he thought, "But there's hell all right. And I'm in it."

He felt dizzy. He had always known his faith was important to him, but only in this moment of doubt did he truly realize *how* important. Who was he apart from his faith? He couldn't even think about that. His whole identity was bound up with believing.

Of course, there were more "practical" questions, too? Could his marriage survive if Mary learned the depth of his doubt? He would certainly have to choose another profession, and nothing else had ever interested him. All those years of preparation wasted! And what would his parents think of him?

But important as those questions were they stayed at the edges of his consciousness. It was his own existence, his soul, that was at stake. He was falling into an abyss.

In the depths of such doubt Thomas could hardly think at all. Yet he did remember that the young Buddhists had talked appreciatively about Prof. David Wilson. And he remembered also that Prof. Wilson was a loyal churchman. At least Wilson might understand what was troubling him. He must talk to someone!

· 10 ·

Prof. Wilson's Study—
Tuesday Afternoon

"You SOUNDED SOMEWHAT AGITATED OVER THE PHONE,"
Prof. Wilson told Thomas. "I hope there's nothing seriously wrong."

"Nothing outwardly wrong, I guess," Thomas answered without conviction, appreciative of the note of
real concern in Wilson's voice, "but inwardly I'm going
through a crisis of faith. I've come to ask your help."

"If I can help, Thomas, I'm at your service. Tell me
what form the crisis is taking with you."

"I've grown up as an orthodox Christian," Thomas answered, "and until recently I've never had any doubts
except about details. Christian faith seemed to make sense
of my community and give me the guidance I needed for
life. But now everything is crashing down around me.
It seems to center on the relation of faith in Christ and
other religions. That's why I've come to you. I've always
believed that Jesus is the one way, the one truth, the one
life — the only path to salvation. That means that we need
to try to win to Christ those who are seeking salvation in
other ways. But now I just don't know."

"What in particular has raised this question for you?"

"Chaplain Levovsky first raised it for me," Thomas answered. "She doesn't want to limit God's presence to Jesus and his followers. What she said seemed so loose I thought she was a heretic. But what has really thrown me is my meeting with the Buddhist fellowship. All they did was tell me their stories, just a couple of them. They turned to Buddhism because they couldn't find what they needed in Christianity! I hadn't thought much before of Christians being converted to other religions. I always thought of conversion as a one-way street. Eventually all would come to Christ. Now it seems that Buddhism has something to offer that Christianity lacks!"

"It's a fine group of young people, isn't it," was Prof. Wilson's reply. "One can't easily dismiss Buddhism as perverse or superstitious. There is so much wisdom there, so much knowledge of how to attain spiritual ends, so much saintliness."

"But if you think Buddhism is just as good as Christianity — or even better — how can you go on being a Christian?" Thomas wondered.

"I don't know that I would want to say just as good or better," Prof. Wilson replied. "I've given up comparisons like that. But let's let that pass for now. The first thing I want you to know is that the problems you're struggling with have been important for me for a long time. The second thing is that we're not alone. There's a large literature written by Christian thinkers on this topic. You don't have to give up faith in Christ in order to appreciate what is positive in other religious traditions."

Thomas brightened. He had read a little about this. At the time it meant very little to him. Perhaps now if he read some of the same essays again they would mean something. "Thanks! Can you tell me how you resolve the issue yourself?"

"There's no simple once-for-all resolution, Thomas, but there is an ongoing discussion — just as in every other area of the church's life and thought. I can tell you a couple of things that have been helpful to me. I decided that one of the problems was the way we often pose the question. We ask, 'Can people find salvation apart from faith in Jesus Christ?' And when we ask that, we suppose we know what we mean by salvation. In the background there is usually some idea of heaven and hell as places we go at death or at the end of history. We want to know whether there's another way that leads to heaven besides our own system of belief."

"Yes, I guess that's how I've thought of it. But how else can we raise the question?"

"Do you think the young Buddhists you talked with are looking for a way to avoid hell and get to heaven?" Dr. Wilson asked.

Thomas thought a moment. "I guess not. They didn't talk about salvation or heaven and hell except as Christian ideas. Alice was looking for mystical experience, or something like that. Bill wanted a religion of tolerance and grace that is sensitive to all sentient beings. That's quite different from what Christians mean by salvation, isn't it?"

"Yes and no," Wilson answered. "Not all Christians are so preoccupied with life after death. Many care a lot about what happens in this life and believe that if we do what we can to serve God here, God will take care of the rest. But the basic point is that people are not all looking for the same thing, and different religious traditions have responded to and shaped different paths to different ends."

"You know, I like that better than the idea of different paths up the same mountain. I don't know why, but I breathe more freely with your image. Maybe there is a sense, an important sense, in which Jesus shows us the one way to 'the Father.' Maybe Hindus and Buddhists are finding ways to something different!"

Prof. Wilson was delighted. "Not many people get the point so quickly! Once I saw that myself, I felt I could study the world religions with complete freedom. I don't ask by what means they try to lead people to salvation. I ask how do they describe the goal and then study how they help people toward it. Of course, just as there is variety among Christians, there is variety in other religious traditions. The overall picture is very complicated."

"Some day I must study that," said Thomas, "but right now it's Jesus I need to understand. The other night a friend of mine was saying that Jesus proclaimed and foreshadowed the coming of the *basileia*, and that that coming is salvation. Would that be one of the Christian views?"

"Surely, and living in anticipation of the coming Realm of God is one meaning of Christian faith," Prof. Wilson replied. "That's quite different from focusing on forgiveness of sin to be found through identification with Jesus' self-sacrifice. And, of course, there are other Christian patterns. Few Eastern Orthodox, for example, would be comfortable with either of these."

"But if Christians don't even agree on what the goal is, how can we talk about Christianity at all. Shouldn't we always say 'Christianities'?"

Prof. Wilson was not quite prepared for that question, but it seemed a good one. "We need to think of Christianity as more inclusive than any doctrine. It seems to be all those movements in human history that have been initiated by those simple but wonderful events in Palestine centering around the person of Jesus. The older I become the more I wonder at the enormous and diverse effects in human history that can be traced to the teachings, the deeds, the death, and the resurrection of that one man."

"I'm glad you mentioned the 'resurrection.'" Thomas knew this was a minor point in Prof. Wilson's comment, but he couldn't let this opportunity pass. "I've always thought that the resurrection is the decisive proof of Jesus' deity. But if so, it would seem to make the salvation effected by Jesus — however we conceive it — radically superior to every other human goal. Can you believe that and still be as appreciative of other religions as you have been?"

"You're a sharp cookie!" Prof. Wilson laughed. "There is no doubt that Christians have often used Jesus' resurrection as a proof of the utter superiority of our faith. Some Christians even denied the resurrection, not because they found it incredible, but because they found the implications drawn from it so offensive. That has been especially true of Christians concerned with the anti-Jewish character of so much Christian teaching.

"Just for that reason I have been delighted by the writing of Rabbi Pinchas Lapide. He's an orthodox Jew with no thought whatever of converting to Christianity. But he believes Jesus rose from the dead — quite literally, and supernaturally. He thinks that was God's way of setting into motion God's mission to carry Jewish truth to the Gentiles. The Jews didn't need it because they already had it."

Thomas was astonished. A Jew could believe in the resurrection of Jesus and remain a Jew! "But what about Hindus and Buddhists?" he asked.

"They wouldn't be likely to think of the resurrection in the same way Rabbi Lapide does. That's partly because they don't make our modern Western distinction between the natural and the supernatural. But in India stories of the extraordinary accomplishments of yogis are very numerous, and there's quite a lot of evidence that many of them are true. If you're brought up in that climate, you're not likely to be incredulous about Jesus' appearance to his disciples after his crucifixion. It would confirm that he was a holy man. It would not lead to picturing him as uniquely superior to all others."

"I can't tell you how much better I feel for having talked with you," said Thomas with enthusiasm. "I'm beginning to see that I can be a Christian and appreciate other traditions at the same time. All these either-ors I've been living with can become both-ands. A week ago if I had heard these same things I would have been upset. But now it feels like the possibility of a new beginning. I'm impatient to get started."

"I'm grateful to you for coming, Thomas" Prof. Wilson replied. "I wish I could help you more on the theological reconstruction. Christology is not my strong suit! And we really don't have any systematic theologians on our university faculty. But it occurs to me that Dr. Cynthia MacDonald might be a good person to talk with. She's the new associate pastor of the congregation to which I belong. She really wants to be a professor, I think, but jobs are scarce, and a campus-related church was the next best thing. Anyway, she told me she's interested in world religions, and I'm sure her degree is in theology. Actually, the senior minister, Dr. James Colletti, would be helpful, too. I seem to recall that he wrote a dissertation on Christology some years ago. What would you say to my inviting you and them over to my home one evening for theological conversation?"

"I would love it," Thomas answered gratefully.

• 11 •

Prof. Wilson's Home—
Friday Evening

Mrs. WILSON MET THOMAS AT THE DOOR and led him into the living room. Prof. Wilson introduced him to Dr. MacDonald with whom he had been chatting. A few minutes later Mrs. Wilson ushered in Dr. Colletti, who was accompanied by a black man much younger than he. Thomas wondered whether he was a college student, but he seemed more mature.

Dr. Colletti introduced the young man to the group. "This is Robert Crawford. He has recently joined our church, and he told me some weeks ago that if there were ever any opportunities for serious theological discussion he would like to be included; so I told him about tonight. I hope no one minds."

They all assured Mr. Crawford that he was welcome. Mrs. Wilson withdrew admitting that she didn't care much for theological discussion. And Prof. Wilson opened the conversation.

"Thomas, here, came to see me quite distressed that his Christology didn't fit with his new experiences. We had a good conversation, but I told him he needed expert counsel. That's why we've invited the two of you."

"Thanks," said Dr. Colletti. "Evenings on theological conversation have never been frequent, but they seem to get rarer. I know I'm rusty, but I'll help if I can. Fortunately, Dr. MacDonald is on top of the newest ideas!"

Dr. MacDonald was a little embarrassed, but she just said, "What's the particular problem, Thomas."

"I went to Prof. Wilson," Thomas explained, "after visiting the Buddhist student group. In talking with them I realized I had nothing to say to them, no reason to offer them to turn to Christ. That made me wonder whether I was a Christian anymore at all. After talking with Prof. Wilson I feel much better. I see it's not a question of giving up my Christian faith but of reconstructing my theology. That's challenging, and I hardly know where to begin. Prof. Wilson thought you could help me."

Dr. MacDonald was intrigued. "How can we help?"

"Well," Thomas answered, "if you believe somehow in the unique nature and importance of Jesus Christ and yet are interested in other religious traditions, I would like to know how you do it. Who was Jesus, and what did he do? What salvation did he bring? That sort of thing."

"I'm not sure I can answer those questions directly," Dr. MacDonald replied. "But I can tell you about a book that shaped my whole approach to theology in the context of religious pluralism. It was written by H. Richard Niebuhr half a century ago now. It's called *The Meaning of Revelation*."

"That's a fine book" Prof. Wilson commented. "It helped me, too, but I had almost forgotten about it. Remind us of Niebuhr's major points."

"Niebuhr distinguishes outer history from inner history. For example, he contrasts the account of the American Revolution in the *Cambridge History* with Lincoln's

Gettysburg Address. Both have their truth. Our inner history provides us with the meanings and values by which we orient ourselves and shape our lives. Outer history provides us with accurate information about the public world. We need to draw facts learned in outer history into our inner history to enrich it and check its distortions."

Thomas was interested, but impatient. "What does that have to do with Christology?"

"We certainly can't build a Christology on that distinction," Dr. MacDonald admitted, "but it does help us to see where Christology comes in. Christians have an inner history, too, the story of the Jewish people and of Christianity as this is remembered and celebrated in the church. For example, we talk about how our forefathers were delivered from slavery in Egypt, even though our blood ancestors may have been in northern Europe at the time. That's quite different from the way secular historians or sociologists write about us. We need to learn from what they tell us, but as believers we'll incorporate that new, and often critical information, into our own story, our inner history.

"The center of our story is Jesus. It is in light of Jesus that we appropriate Jewish history as our own. And it is in light of Jesus that we read about his followers and appraise the history of the church. For us Jesus is the basis for all our judgments of meaning and value."

"And is that what you mean by calling Jesus the revelation of God?" Thomas wanted to know.

"Yes, it is. The longer I live with Niebuhr's way of putting it, the truer it seems to me. I keep learning to remember the story differently. Elements that were once important have drifted into the background, and others have come forth as crucial. Women play a much larger role than they once did in my Christian story. But I find that each change I make is determined by the centrality of Jesus. And the unity of the whole I find in him."

This was too much to grasp all at once, but Thomas saw promise in the idea. "What does that mean in relation to other religions. Should I have tried to get those Buddhist students to look at everything in the light of Jesus?"

"That might be okay," replied Dr. MacDonald, "but that's not Niebuhr's point. To take an analogy, we live by an inner history as a nation, too, but we know that other nations live by different inner histories. We can tell them our story, and we should listen to theirs. We're not trying to get them to use ours. I think for Niebuhr the same is true for us as Christians, at least initially. We should tell our story to all who will listen. We'll be very pleased if others join our community by appropriating our story as their own. But conversion is not what it's all about. It has more to do with understanding one another and learning from one another. We need to hear their stories, too."

"Does that mean that we assume that there are many paths up the same mountain?" Thomas asked.

"I think Niebuhr leaves that an open question," said Dr. MacDonald. Maybe so, maybe not. We can only find out by listening. The main point is that the revelatory power of Jesus does not predetermine the truth or falsity of other inner histories. They may or may not have revelatory centers. We can witness passionately and confidently to the truth of our faith while leaving completely open the truth of other faiths. That's what I find so liberating."

Dr. Colletti entered the discussion. "I appreciate your enthusiasm for that book, Cynthia. It gives us a way to speak fully and honestly about the work of Jesus without implying anything pejorative about other communities of faith. That's a great achievement. But Niebuhr doesn't help when we ask about the person of Jesus. I've always thought that was the Christological question par excellence. How are you thinking about this, Thomas?"

"In the past, Dr. Colletti, I've tried to keep the person

and work together. I've begun with a theory of the atonement, like Anselm's, that requires that the savior be both God and a human being. So I've stressed the utter supernatural uniqueness of Jesus' person. Recently I've become much less sure of all that. Most of the people I've talked to don't think of Jesus' work in Anselm's way as paying the price of human sin, and other ideas do seem at least as fruitful. But I need a lot of help. If we think of Jesus' work apart from traditional atonement theory, what happens to the doctrine of Jesus' person?"

"That's a big topic," Dr. Colletti answered. "I knew the literature quite thoroughly once — when I was writing my dissertation, but I'm much fuzzier now and out of date besides. My main conclusion was that there is indeed a close connection between ways of thinking of Jesus' work and person. But my thesis was that every way of speaking of Jesus' work that was at all adequate to Christian faith required a way of thinking of Jesus' person that generally followed the Chalcedonian pattern. Jesus is both divine and human."

Thomas found that reassuring in a way but troubling in another. "But if we affirm Jesus' deity, don't we give up the open-endedness with regard to other religions? Or do we allow that their founders may also have been God?"

"My opinion," Dr. Colletti replied, "is that, depending on the view of Jesus' work, there can be affirmations of Jesus' divinity that leave us quite open to hearing the claims of other religious traditions without prejudging them. But there is one point in your formulation to which I object. You seem to imply that to assert Jesus' divinity is to assert that Jesus was God. Many people think that is an orthodox doctrine. Maybe it is, but I don't believe it, and I want you to know that's *not* what I'm calling for."

Thomas was startled. Dr. Colletti had sounded quite orthodox, and yet now he was heatedly denying that Jesus was God. "But what can it mean to affirm Jesus' divinity if not that Jesus was God incarnate."

Dr. Colletti was ready for that one. "To me there is a big difference between saying that Jesus is God incarnate and saying that Jesus is the incarnation of God. 'God incarnate' sounds like God has taken on human form while remaining God. That's certainly the way a lot of Christians have thought and taught. But as I studied the Christological councils, it seemed to me that notion was rejected. Jesus was a truly human being in whom God was incarnate."

Thomas remembered now Prof. O'Connor's explanation. She had distinguished the Logos assuming humanity from the Logos dwelling in a human being. She had been more neutral between the two images than was Dr. Colletti. But at least Thomas got the idea. To say that Jesus was the truly human being in whom God was incarnate was more like saying Jesus was the man in whom God dwelt. He wondered whether Dr. Colletti liked Donald Baillie's formulation. "Do you like Baillie's idea of modeling the paradox of incarnation on the paradox of grace?" he asked.

"Yes, I do, although I can't follow all of what Baillie says. He seems to assume that Jesus, the real historical man, was always perfect. But our historical knowledge can't possibly support such extreme views and it's pointless to bring faith in to fill gaps in historical knowledge. We don't know enough about Jesus to specify his 'sins' or 'imperfections,' but we certainly don't know enough about him to deny that he had any. At that point we moderns simply have to part company with the early church fathers."

A sinful Jesus, Thomas thought, now I've heard everything! Yet Dr. Colletti seemed really to care to get the old puzzle of the unity of the deity and the humanity straight. Thomas was genuinely puzzled. "If you follow Baillie in general and then say that Jesus was imperfect, there's not much difference between Jesus and ourselves, is there?"

"If you think of the difference as a matter of degree, you're quite right, Thomas," Dr. Colletti replied. "I don't think Baillie meant to do that, but he didn't make it clear how we can avoid it. When I read about Jesus in the New Testament, he seems different from me. And the difference doesn't seem to be just that he was wiser or more loving or more in tune with God — though all of that seems to be true, too."

"What is the difference, then?" Thomas asked.

"Jesus seems more like the prophets than like me. He seems to know what God wills and wants to say without learning it from books. Yet there's a difference there, too. The prophets pass on the word they receive from God. Jesus speaks for God out of his own immediate awareness. God is present in all of us, no doubt, but even St. Paul did not speak as Jesus did. He experienced some kind of struggle between his own self and God working in him as 'Christ' or 'Spirit.'" Jesus sometimes struggled with himself as in the Garden of Gethsemane. But much of the time God's presence in him seemed to be one with his very selfhood. I think that's what the creeds are saying — or should be saying, if they aren't."

"That's an interesting speculation, Dr. Colletti," interjected Dr. MacDonald. "but does it really make any difference what was going on in the interior of Jesus' experience? Isn't it what Jesus does for us that matters — and that only? And doesn't that depend on how he was perceived and imaged rather than on Jesus' private life with God? I've been persuaded by those who say we just can't know enough about him historically to make those judgments. We *can* be sure that believers found God in him, but I don't see how we can say more than that."

"You may be right," Dr. Colletti replied, "but I've never

been satisfied with that position. I think it has always been important to Christians to believe that God was really acting differently in Jesus. It hasn't been enough to know that believers were specially affected by him. Indeed, I'm not sure the effects would have occurred as they did apart from the belief about how God was acting in Jesus himself. Even today, if we give up on the doctrine of the person of Jesus, I wonder whether we will continue to accord his teaching and his deeds the full authority they deserve."

"Thomas," Prof. Wilson broke in, "I think you can see why I wanted you to talk with the theologians. Even they can't agree, and these mysteries are quite beyond me. I like to say I'm a historian and don't have to come to my own conclusions. I do like to see how similar issues arise in different religious traditions. For example, Buddhist orthodoxy is quite opposite to Christian orthodoxy on the analogous point. It insists that Gautama was a human being and that we can all be enlightened just as he was. But Buddhists throughout the centuries have been enormously impressed by the difference. In their eyes Gautama became something incomprehensibly superior to them. And I don't think that should be dismissed as a popular superstition either."

"Are you saying that Gautama is also an incarnation of God, just like Jesus?" Thomas pressed him.

"No, I don't think so. As a historian I like to see parallels but not to set the differences aside. The Buddhists say Gautama was a Buddha, that is, an Enlightened One. I think they are right. I've tried thinking of Jesus as another Enlightened One. Many Buddhists would be happy to see him that way. But for me it doesn't work. I prefer to stick with the incarnation of God in Jesus' case. But similarly I prefer to think of Gautama as the Buddhists do — as the Enlightened One."

"You mean that Buddhists are right about Gautama and

Christians are right about Jesus?" Dr. MacDonald asked. "I like that. And perhaps Hindus are right about Krishna, and Muslims, about Mohammed! So we can all live and let live in mutual appreciation."

"I want to live and let live in mutual appreciation," Dr. Colletti agreed, "but I don't want that to mean we just leave each other alone. If Gautama was really enlightened, and if enlightenment is as valuable as it seems to be, I want Christians to learn more about it from the Buddhists. The Catholics are way ahead of us here. They're practicing Buddhist meditation techniques on a wide scale. I gather Thomas Merton led the way in this country. Most of the Protestants who are appreciative of Buddhism just talk about it."

"But is it just a matter of learning from the Buddhists?" Thomas asked. "Don't we have something to teach?"

"Indeed, I think we do," Dr. Colletti answered. "Our task is to understand both our faith and Buddhism well enough to know what we do have to offer. We need a lot more dialogue. My own impression is that our gospel can have great meaning for Buddhists if it can be freed from some of the Western forms we have fastened on it."

"One area in which we have a lot to share," Dr. Mac-Donald added, "is in the social sphere. I don't know a lot about Buddhism, I admit, but so far it has seemed to me to focus very much on the interior lives of individuals. I have been excited by Latin American liberation theology, and I doubt that anything like that will come out of Buddhism unless Buddhists are influenced by Christianity. To me it has become very important to see that Jesus identified with the poor and calls on us to identify with the oppressed of our day. In the context of the real world, that may be more important than the qualities of inner life attained through Buddhist meditation. But Prof. Wilson knows a lot more about these matters than I do!"

Prof. Wilson felt free at this point to make a confession of his own faith. "I may have studied Buddhism and other religious traditions more than the rest of you, but I'm still a novice and a generalist. Yet I do have my own convictions. I am sure that Christians have a lot to learn from others, and especially from Buddhists, perhaps. I think right now that learning from them may be more important than trying to teach them. We've done a lot of that — often quite insensitively — and we've generated a lot of legitimate resentment. Too often we've used the technological, economic, and even military power of Christendom to push Christian ideas on people.

"But when all is said and done, I believe that when our lives and understanding are centered in Jesus Christ, we *can* incorporate the truth the others have to offer. I'm not sure that the others have a center from which they can incorporate one another's truths and ours. That's why I think that one day, if history goes on long enough, and if we Christians can get out of the way, every knee will bow at the name of Jesus!"

"Wow," said Thomas. "I've said that often enough, but it sounds quite different when you say it. It doesn't mean that I should have been able to convert those Buddhist young people back to Christianity. Maybe I need to be more concerned about the conversion of Christianity away from its narrowness. Maybe the spread of Buddhist practices in the West will even be of help to Christians!"

"That's certainly the way I feel," said Prof. Wilson. "Frankly those Buddhists seem to be making a greater contribution to God's total work in the world than most of the Christians I know. I support them as much as I can. That seems to be Chaplain Levovsky's policy, too. She's a courageous woman.

"By the way, Mr. Crawford, you've been very quiet. What do you think of all this?"

"It's hard to say," Mr. Crawford answered after a pause. "It all sounds so theoretical. It's not the kind of thing that drew me to Christ and finally led me to join the church."

Mr. Crawford had their attention. Thomas was especially eager to hear more. "What did attract you?" he asked.

"I guess the only way of answering that is to tell you something of my life history," Mr. Crawford answered smiling. "Well, I was brought up by a skeptical father and a pious mother. Mother sometimes took me to church with her, but I imbibed my father's attitudes. Really Christianity was not an important issue to me.

"The first time I lived away from home was when I came to this college. Like a lot of fellows away from home for the first time I lived quite self-indulgently. Then in my senior year I took a course in religion — more because of when it was offered than because of any special interest. It was on the teachings of Jesus, and it was taught in a very academic style. But still it made me read, and what I read grabbed me. To live that life would mean changing everything. It would mean putting others before myself, and caring especially for the disadvantaged.

"It's particular implications for me were all too clear. I would have to stop trying to make as many girls as I could; I would have to become frugal with my money, giving all I could to meet urgent human needs; I could no longer take pleasure in the way my country bullied smaller ones; and there was this quite unpopular sophomore I would have to befriend.

"Most of my classmates just treated all this as an academic exercise, and they kept on living as they had before. I also found that even quite serious Christians paid rather little attention to Jesus' teaching. But to me the challenge was clear. Jesus had meant it and had lived it all the way, even to the cross. I had to try to live it too."

"Was it because Jesus seemed to you divine that you felt you must obey him?" Thomas wanted to know.

"No, it wasn't like that," Mr. Crawford answered. "It was more that his words convinced and convicted me. I didn't think much about whether he was divine or not. But later I accepted the idea of his divinity — without much reflection — because of the power and truth of what he taught."

Thomas was moved. "How has your commitment to Jesus worked out?" he asked.

"During the rest of that senior year it was quite spotty. Sometimes I lived the Jesus-way; sometimes I fell back into my old patterns. I think I would have lost the battle had I not met Ted Hirsch. He had been a committed Christian for several years, and he introduced me to his friends who lived with him in a commune. After graduation I moved in with them. Only two of us work for pay. Since we live frugally, they support the rest of us so that we can work with the youth in the slums. It's rough, but we're making a little progress against dope and prostitution and gangs."

"That is a different world from the one we've been talking about tonight, isn't it?" Pastor Colletti commented gently and a bit ruefully. "Why were you so eager to join us?"

"For the first months after I entered the commune," Mr. Crawford replied, "I thought the one thing needful was to live the Jesus-way. But gradually life became more complicated. There are six of us living together in rather close quarters, and despite our shared commitment we often get on one another's nerves. We try hard to work the problems out by being honest and acknowledging our faults. But we've begun to see that we've been trying to do it all by good works and that there's more to Christianity than that. We used to ridicule those who talked about justification by faith because that talk seemed to be an excuse for them not to take Jesus' call to discipleship seriously. We don't anymore. We're sure grace is important, but we don't understand that very well.

"Then in trying to help slum youth to find another way to live, we've been forced to recognize how little freedom they have. Given the attitudes of middle-class people, the economic structures of society, the way political power is exercised, and the despair of the adults around them, I sometimes marvel that they survive at all. Indeed, many don't. We used to think all they needed was to decide to live the Jesus-way and to shape up. Now we're beginning to think that their salvation depends on some changes elsewhere in society as well. And we know that these are issues that have been thought about a lot in the church.

"In short, we are realizing that there's more to being Christian than we first thought and that theology is important. That led me to stop being contemptuous of the church for its lukewarmness and its compromises and to join it myself. But just going to church and hearing sermons — sorry, Dr. Colletti — doesn't get me very far. I thought tonight might be different."

The group fell silent, sobered by its recognition that tonight had not been very different — at least in relation to Mr. Crawford's burning issues. Dr. Colletti finally broke the silence. "Theology is a complex business, isn't it. So many questions! Tonight we came to talk about Thomas's problems. They are very real to him — and to us, too. I think what we've said has some bearing on your problems, Mr. Crawford, but we certainly have not made that relevance clear. What say we all meet at my home a week from tonight for another conversation?"

All agreed and the group broke up. Thomas went to Mr. Crawford to have a personal word with him. He had been deeply moved. The kind of radical discipleship Mr. Crawford was trying to live out had been foreign to his world.

In his conservative home church it would have been dismissed as fanaticism. But when he heard Mr. Crawford speak, he knew it should not be dismissed. If Mr. Crawford had been with those Buddhist youth, he could have given a testimony that would have touched them, Thomas thought a bit enviously. "Could I visit your group and see something of your work?" he asked. They made plans, and Thomas went home, filled with excitement.

• 12 •

At Home—Late Friday Night

Mary OPENED THE DOOR when she heard Thomas fumbling with his key. She was getting sleepy, but when she saw Thomas she knew they needed to talk. He was far too excited to sleep. It was time for de-briefing.

"You look happier than you have for some time," she said. "I'm so glad."

"Yes, I feel as though a great weight has been lifted, although I can't really say what it is. Maybe it's that I was feeling the need to defend Christ, and now I feel that Christ can take care of himself."

"Does that mean that you got answers to the questions that were troubling you, darling?" Mary wanted to know.

"That's hard to say, sweetheart. I've heard lots and lots of answers. But every answer just raises new questions. I still don't know where it will all lead."

"But you do feel better about things, don't you?" Mary was troubled by Thomas's answer but still reassured by his expression.

"Oh, yes, indeed!" Thomas replied enthusiastically. "For a while I felt that everything was falling apart. Now I feel as though doors are opening and hands are beckoning. I'm really eager to get back to the books. I think I'll

81

understand what the theologians are saying much better now."

"Can you tell me some of the things you've learned?" Mary asked. "I know I can't catch up on all of it, but I don't want to be left completely behind."

Thomas was deeply grateful for her attitude. Even in his exaltation he had been dreading the growing gap between the way she thought and the new ideas he was wanting to pursue. He understood all too well how she thought and how much sense it made to think that way. "I would like to try," he said. "But it's not going to be easy. It sure hasn't been easy for me! I'm glad you heard the discussion here the other night. That gives you an idea. I've heard more talk about Baillie tonight. I guess the biggest problem for me was how to think of Jesus Christ in the face of my experience with those Buddhist students. You know how upset I was about my inability to witness to them. I just couldn't imagine how I could really believe in Jesus Christ and then not have anything to say when Buddhists asked me to tell them! Tonight I decided that it was all right that I couldn't tell them they were wrong. I can really and truly believe in Jesus and still respect and admire what they're doing — and not try to redirect them back to the church — not now at any rate."

"Well, I'm glad you feel better, but I'll have to admit I worry that you may be losing your moorings. If Jesus is God's saving Word to all people, don't those young people need to hear it, too?"

Thomas tried to explain what Prof. Wilson had said. In the context of the earlier conversation it had made a lot of sense. Without that context it was not reassuring to Mary. She became genuinely concerned about Thomas's new theological development. Had he, after all, abandoned the orthodox faith?

"Darling," she said at last, "I'm confused, and I think

you're a bit confused, too. I'm also worried for you. I admit it. Some of what you say doesn't sound Christian to me. I don't see why we need to learn from Buddhists when we already have God's Word in the Bible. But I won't make an issue of that. Let's get back to basics. Do you believe that Jesus Christ is your one Lord and Savior?"

Thomas was sobered by that. It wasn't fair, he felt, to have to answer yes or no to that kind of question. But only a couple of weeks earlier he would have thought it a very correct question indeed. He would have thought that all the elaborations were evasions of the simplest and most unequivocal issue. And Mary, of course, thought so now. Why should she not? And besides, maybe she was right. Maybe his hesitation *was* an evasion. She wanted to know about his personal faith, not his theology. Had his commitment remained firm? Was he ready to serve Jesus wholeheartedly, without reservations? Was he?

"Yes," Thomas finally answered. "Jesus Christ is my one Lord and Savior. That may not mean quite the same thing to me it once did. But I think it means more, not less. Now I see that Jesus saves me from the need to cling to a particular theology, that he frees me to be open to new ideas — to truth wherever it is. I'm excited by that. I think I understand why his yoke is easy and his burden is light, how he is truly life and light and the way for me to follow. I feel that the Spirit he gave is with me as I've never felt it before. I feel free to love everyone, whatever they believe. I don't need to defend Christianity anymore. Its truth will win the day and the chaff, of which there has been so much, will blow away.

"But something else happened tonight, Mary. There was a young man there who takes Jesus' teaching more seriously than anyone I have met before. He made me see that affirming Jesus as Lord is not primarily a matter of beliefs but rather discipleship. I don't see how I can ever follow Jesus as literally as he does, but I'm going to try somehow to shape my life in the way Jesus taught. I'm scared of what that will mean. But I'm also excited. Yes, yes, indeed!" It came to him almost as a revelation. "Jesus Christ *is* my one Lord and Savior!"

"Then I thank God, darling," Mary sighed. "Let's go to bed."

• 13 •

Discussion Guide

CHRISTOLOGY IS CENTRAL to all Christian theology. It can be subdivided into numerous topics including Jesus' pre-existence, his birth, his teaching, his miracles, his atoning death, his resurrection, his ascension, his coming again, his relation to the Father and to the Spirit, the relation of the historical Jesus to the Christ of faith, the Kingdom he proclaimed, his royal, priestly, and prophetic offices, and so forth. Only a few of these topics are touched on in the story. The focus there is on the person of Jesus, specifically the relation of his divinity to his humanity. Other topics are touched on peripherally.

Similarly, questions about Christology can be raised from the point of view of a variety of contemporary concerns. Liberation theology has lifted to primacy Jesus' role as liberator, understanding this as prominently including economic and political aspects. On the other hand, there is a continuing tradition that focuses on personal sin as the single crucial problem and asks how Jesus is effective in mediating forgiveness. There are others who understand religion in more mystical terms and ask how a contingent historical event can be relevant. In this book the primary questioning is from the point of view of religious pluralism with secondary attention to feminist concerns.

This is simply to acknowledge the limitations of this book as an introduction to Christology. Nevertheless, the issues that are raised are central ones in our time, and ones that are likely to arise in the minds of many contemporary Christians. The purpose of this study guide is to encourage frank discussion of this limited but important range of questions about Christology. Throughout, the suggested questions follow the sequence of the text.

Chapters 1–4
These four chapters are designed to raise the issue of whether belief in Jesus' unique deity is necessary for Christian faith. One question is proposed for each of the four chapters.

1. If Chaplain Levovsky thinks of Jesus only as a human being, do you agree with Thomas that she is not a Christian? If so why? What is so important about Jesus' divinity?

2. Do you find some of the traditional Christian dogma repelling? Do you know people who reject Christianity on their account? Do you know anyone whose confession of faith would be similar to Chaplain Levovsky's? Do you consider that person a Christian?

3. Can a purely human Jesus be a place for people to begin a pilgrimage of faith? Or should that kind of thinking be denounced as heresy?

4. In asking who Jesus is, does it make sense to start with the experience of a particular people and inquire how Jesus is good news for them? Or should we begin with church teaching and judge culture by that? Is the idea that God is like Jesus a good starting point for theology?

Chapter 5

This chapter is designed to introduce something of the history through which orthodox Christology was fashioned. It also presents a way of understanding Christianity as a historical movement through which the Spirit of God is progressively expressed. The purpose is to suggest alternative ways of viewing the authority of tradition.

1. Does Arianism make sense to you? If it had triumphed politically and remained "orthodox," would you be able to be orthodox today?

2. Does the historical success of a doctrine signal God's approval?

3. Can you distinguish between the Logos assuming humanity and the Logos dwelling in a human being? Which is closer to your way of thinking?

4. Was Nestorius wrong to deny that Mary was the Mother of God?

5. Should we accept the great creeds of the church even when we do not understand them?

6. Do you think Orthodox Christology has encouraged Christians to be anti-Jewish?

7. Can we trust the Spirit working through the church to bring us to truth, or do we need restrictions on what ideas can be introduced into the discussion?

8. Should the church's Christological teaching be tested against the results of contemporary New Testament scholarship? If this is done how well will it fare?

Chapter 6

This chapter provides an opportunity to see how one version of liberal Christianity understands itself. This kind of thinking has at times been quite widespread in some sections of Protestantism. There have also been sharp reactions against it.

1. If we thought of Jesus' divinity in terms of the Holy Spirit's special presence in him, instead of that of the Logos, would that make a significant difference?

2. Do you think of Jesus as differing from us in kind or in degree?

3. Can a Christian believe that God was present in great leaders of other religious traditions?

4. Is the main purpose of foreign missions to gain converts to Christianity or to serve the total needs of people in other countries? Does it make sense to cooperate with other religious communities in serving the people?

Chapter 7

Here we relate to our discussion the questions recently raised by feminist Christians. Among feminists the question of whether they can remain Christians or must become post-Christians is a seriously debated one. Of course, Christology is only one of the problems with which they deal.

1. Do you see any problem for women in the fact that Jesus was a man? If you do, are any of the proposed answers helpful?

2. Do you think of salvation as something the Christian already knows in relation to Christ or as something promised and yet to come for which the Christian hopes?

3. Do you think of divinity and humanity as so related that the more Jesus is divine the *less* he is human? Or do you think of them as so related that the more Jesus is divine the *more* he is human?

4. Does it make sense to you that God is *in* human beings? Or do you prefer to think of God as present *to* you?

Chapter 8
This a pause in the story giving Thomas a chance to reflect. The questions he asks himself constitute a summary of the kinds of questions raised thus far in this Discussion Guide. They will be a good basis for review at this point.

Chapter 9
Instead of just having Christians talk about other religious traditions, chapter 9 allows some Buddhists to speak for themselves. As this challenges Thomas to respond, it should also challenge Christian readers.

1. Do you believe that Buddhists have authentic religious experience? If so, is it the same as that of Christians? If it is different, how?

2. Can Buddhism be an avenue of salvation?

3. If you had Thomas's chance to make a Christian witness to these Buddhists, what would you have said? Does it make sense to affirm that Jesus Christ is the one Savior of the world in conversation with those who are finding religious meaning in Buddhism?

Chapter 10
Chapter 10 provides a discussion of how Christians can respond to Buddhists and others without either condemning them or renouncing their own claims. In a world in

which Christians are more and more interacting with followers of other religious ways, this becomes increasingly
important. Of course, only a few of the many possible
theological responses are mentioned.

1. Are all religious ways paths to the same end, or do
   they lead to different goals?

2. If Christians have differing ideas about the goal, is
   only one group correct?

3. Does the resurrection of Jesus prove the superiority
   of Christianity?

4. Could one believe that Jesus rose from the dead and
   not be a Christian?

5. How do you personally interpret the religious meaning of non-Christian traditions?

Chapters 11-12
These chapters present a direct discussion of central Christological issues in light of considerations raised in previous
chapters. Here, too, only a few of the positions now being
discussed in theological circles are presented. The reader
not satisfied with the directions here pursued is encouraged to enter the contemporary discussion.

1. Does the distinction between inner history and outer
   history make sense? Is Jesus the center of your inner
   history?

2. Are you interested in hearing the inner histories of
   Jews, Muslims, Hindus, and others? Do you think
   you may learn something of importance from them?

3. Anselm taught that God became a human being in
   order that a human being could pay the debt owed

by humanity to God for sin. Does that view of atonement satisfy you?

4. Does Jesus' "divinity" mean to you that Jesus was God?

5. Does the distinction between Jesus as God incarnate and Jesus as the incarnation of God make sense? Which idea do you prefer?

6. Is it important to you to believe that Jesus was perfect? Why?

7. Does Dr. Colletti's way of seeing Jesus as different from us in kind rather than degree make sense to you? Does it make any difference?

8. Can you agree that in relation to other religious traditions Christians should both listen and witness?

9. Can Jesus Christ be the center of an inner history that is informed by the contributions of all traditions?

10. What is the relation between doctrines about Jesus and practical discipleship? Are other doctrines more important?

11. Do you see the changes in Thomas as growth in faith or as loss of firm moorings?

Suggested Reading

Baillie, Donald M. *God Was in Christ*. New York: Macmillan, 1948. A devout meditation on the history of reflection about the natures of Jesus and his work. It offers a constructive proposal for thinking of the incarnation as the perfect act of grace.

Berkouwer, C. G. *The Person of Christ*, trans. by John Vriend. Grand Rapids, Mich.: Eerdmans, 1954. An authoritative statement of conservative Christology in the Reformed tradition.

Boff, Leonardo. *Jesus Christ Liberator*. Maryknoll, N.Y.: Orbis, 1978. A major reformulation of traditional Christology from the point of view of Latin American liberation theology.

Bornkamm, Gunter. *Jesus of Nazareth*, trans. by Irene and Fraser McLuskey with James Robinson. New York: Harper & Row, 1960. A major New Testament scholar explains what modern scholarship allows us to say with some confidence about the life and message of the historical Jesus.

Brock, Rita Nakashima. *Journey by Heart: A Christology of Erotic Power*. New York: Crossroad, 1988. A radical feminist undertakes an affirmative and moving statement about Christ.

Davis, Stephen. *Encountering Jesus*. Atlanta: John Knox Press, 1988. Five theologians, ranging from conservative evangelical to radical, present their views, criticize one another, and then defend themselves against the criticism. There is also a Jewish response to the discussion.

Driver, Tom E. *Christ in a Changing World*. New York: Crossroad, 1981. A sustained argument against attributing any uniqueness to Jesus Christ that leads to claims of superiority over others.

Herzog, Frederick. *God-Walk: Liberation Shaping Dogmatics.* Maryknoll, N.Y.: Orbis, 1988. A passionate argument that Christology should be transformed in terms of Christopraxis, which means radical discipleship.

Lapide, Pinchas. *The Resurrection of Jesus,* trans. by Wilhelm C. Linss. Minneapolis: Augsburg, 1983. An orthodox Jew strongly defends the resurrection of Jesus and interprets it as God's way of inaugurating the mission to the Gentiles.

Niebuhr, H. Richard. *The Meaning of Revelation.* New York: Macmillan, 1941. A now classic statement of confessional theology that turns historical relativism into a positive basis for affirming the centrality of Jesus Christ.

Pittenger, Norman. *Christology Reconsidered.* London: SCM Press, 1970. Readable reflections on Jesus Christ by a historian who makes use of the categories of process thought.

Robinson, John A. T. *The Human Face of God.* Philadelphia: Westminster, 1973. The English bishop, author of the best-selling *Honest to God,* develops the implications of his radical theology for how Jesus is to be understood by Christians.

Index